CONTENT AREA READING: A PRACTICAL GUIDE

CONTENT AREA READING: A PRACTICAL GUIDE

BY
PAULA WITKOWSKI
DIANNE SWENSON KOEHNECKE

✸*ENROUTE*

ENROUTE
5705 Rhodes Avenue
St. Louis, MO 63109
Contact us at contactus@enroutebooksandmedia.com

Cover by TJ Burdick
Cover credit: stock photo

Library of Congress Control Number: 2018951526

Copyright © 2018 Paula Witkowski & Dianne Swenson Koehnecke
All rights reserved.

Print ISBN-13: 978-1-7324148-4-6
Print ISBN-10: 1-7324148-4-X
E-book ISBN-13: 978-1-7324148-6-0
E-book ISBN-10: 1-7324148-6-6

Printed in the United States of America
1 3 5 7 9 10 8 6 4 2

CONTENTS

HOW TO USE THIS TEXTBOOK — i

CHAPTER ONE: GETTING STARTED — 1

   Introduction — 1
   What Good Teachers Do — 3
   What Good Readers Do — 4
   Evidence & Accountability — 5
   Dealing with Motivation — 7
   Lesson Plan Guide/Unit Plan Guide — 8
   Summary — 8
   References — 9

ESSENTIAL ELEMENTS FOR ALL CONTENT AREAS: FRAMEWORK TARGETING BEFORE, DURING, & AFTER READING — 11

CHAPTER TWO: BEFORE READING — 13

   Know the Text — 14
   Survey, Skim, & Scan — 15
   Build Background Knowledge — 15
   Graphic Organizers — 16
   Preview Vocabulary — 18
   Word Consciousness — 19
   Provide a Purpose for Reading — 21
   Summary — 22
   References — 23

CHAPTER THREE: DURING READING — 25

   Dealing with Vocabulary — 26
   Reading Guides — 26
   Empty Outlines — 29
   Questioning — 29
   Collaboration/Group Investigations — 30
   Graphic Organizers — 32
   Thinking Aloud — 33
   Formative Assessments — 34
   Summary — 34
   References — 35

CHAPTER FOUR: AFTER READING — 37

   Exit Slips — 38
   Writing Process — 38
   RAFT Writing — 39
   Questioning the Author — 40
   KWL — 41
   Response Writing — 41
   Poetry Writing — 42
   Mnemonics — 43

Summary	44
References	45

CHAPTER FIVE: 47
THE LANGUAGES OF CONTENT AREA- VOCABULARY

English/Language Arts, Social Studies, Music	48
Math	49
English Language Learners	50
Foreign Languages	51
Special Education	52
Art	53
Science	54
Useful Websites	56
Answers	56
Summary	56
References	57

CHAPTER SIX: READABILITY LEVELS 59

Reading Levels: Independent, Instructional, and Frustration	59
Lexile Formula	60
Fry Formula	60
Flesch-Kinkaid Formula	62
Checklists	65
WISC Acronym for Readability Checklist	66
Checklist for WISC Acronym	66
Summary	67

Useful Websites	68
References	69

CHAPTER SEVEN: 71
DIFFERENTIATION TO MEET THE NEEDS OF ALL STUDENTS

Differentiated Instruction	71
Struggling Readers	74
What Can Be Done?	78
Assessment Issues	79
Summary	81
References	82

CHAPTER EIGHT: 83
USING TRADE BOOKS IN ALL CONTENT AREAS

Educational Goals and Expectations	84
The Phenomena of Harry Potter	85
Important Theorists for Today's Readers	86
Useful Websites	86
Graphic Novels	88
Reluctant Readers	88
Children's Books	89
Genres	94
Useful Reading Strategies	94
Criteria for Choosing Young Adult Books	96
Summary	96
Useful Guides	96

References	98

CHAPTER NINE: MEDIA LITERACY: THE NEW LITERACIES — 101

All Students have Literacy Strengths	102
Evidence Based Research Supports The Use of Digital Literacies	103
Summary	109
Useful Media Literacy Websites	109
References	110

CHAPTER TEN: STEM AND STEAM PRACTICE IN THE CLASSROOM — 111

STEM	111
STEAM	113
Summary	114
References	115

CHAPTER ELEVEN: PUTTING IT ALL TOGETHER — 117

National Standards, State Standards, School District Standards, Core Curriculum Standards	118
Literacy Coaches	118
Summary	119
References	120

APPENDIX — 123

A. Interviews	123

HOW TO READ THIS BOOK
(PREFACE)

Choose your own chapters

When you read an eBook that is a textbook we have several suggestions to make your process flow much more smoothly. First, make sure you read the preface to make sure you know why the authors wrote the book. Neither Dianne nor Paula read the preface when they were in college. Only when they became teachers themselves and were selecting text books for their students did they realize how important the preface is in selecting a particular book because **the author explains not only the purpose for writing the book but also why it can be helpful to students.** Whenever text books are revised it is also important to see if any important changes have been made.

Useful Tips

As a student, you may not be able to choose your own text books but it can still be useful to read the preface. After you read the preface, skim through the table of contents. **Pick out chapters that you think will be interesting, new, or difficult.** Now you have already set a purpose for what you will be reading.

Goal

The three S's: **survey, scan and skim** are also useful when you first review the textbook. **Get an overview of each chapter. This your survey.** The scanning occurs when you review headings, subheadings, and the graphic elements. In the skimming phase you turn every subhead into a question and then you quickly read to find an answer to the question. Good textbooks will usually have an introduction and a summary even though they may not be labeled as such.

Survey, Skim & Scan

Interact

When first reading each, **feel free to highlight and make notes in the margins.** Read the beginning and ending carefully, see if you can then put the main ideas in your own words by writing, mapping, or illustrating. This strategy need not be a physical representation; instead it can be metacognitive where you are thinking about the highlights in the chapter. If chapters have summaries, read them first.

Review

When reading the chapter more thoroughly you can take time to review web links, charts and other visual aids, questions or any other prompt that helps you understand and apply what you have read. **Another good idea is to review the chapter again just before you go into a class and before a quiz or exam.** If you try to read everything just before an exam you may well ace the exam but you won't remember a thing you read.

The more you interact with the text, question the author, think about what you've read, discuss the content and come back to the book months or even years later and remember what you've learned and applied, you have become **a proficient, skilled, and professional reader.**

CHAPTER ONE
GETTING STARTED

INTRODUCTION

We all want to be 'great' teachers, don't we? But it's not as easy as some might think. Dealing with a variety of learners—those who are academically gifted, those who struggle with learning, and those who come from a variety of different backgrounds and cultures—takes a great deal of practice, preparation, and planning. Don't despair though. This text will help all teachers in all subject areas become better at what they do—to be great! We provide a framework for teaching content subjects that we've found to work well with all learners.

Middle and High School students who struggle with reading usually fall into one of three groups (Schoenbach, Greenleaf, Cziko, & Hurwitz, 1999).

The first group has major deficiencies in reading that stem from never having learned decoding skills. The second group generally understands enough phonics to painstakingly sound out words. Unfortunately, these students become so intent on decoding, they lose any sense of the meaning of the words and sentences. The third group, and by far the largest, is composed of students who do not have poor decoding skills or little or no understanding of phonics. Instead, these students have limited vocabularies and a lack of basic background knowledge to apply to their reading, which means they cannot comprehend at the necessary level. Unfortunately, students in this category are usually not recognized as struggling readers by content area teachers in middle and high school classrooms throughout the United States.

Statistics indicate that young adults today, at least in our country, are not keeping up with the demands of current literacy trends. The data also highlights disparities between racial and ethnic groups and among students coming from different socio-economic levels. For example, reading scores of 12th grade students on the National Assessment of Educational Progress (NAEP) have remained static for the past 20 years (Darwin and Fleischman, April 2005, p. 85). For over 25 years, the gap between the scores of white and black students has widened in 8th and 12th grade (U.S. Department of Education, 2000). Yet most teachers of middle and high school students continue to use textbooks as the major printed source of their content areas, even when the average student in secondary classrooms reads below the level of many content area texts (Allington, 2002).

The way many teachers compensate for the students who cannot read their textbooks is often by using the lecture method to help the students with key ideas and concepts (Darwin and Fleischman, p. 85). Unfortunately, the lecture method can thwart the students' needs for improving their literacy skills, because instead of addressing the problem, it merely avoids it (Schoenback et al., 1999).

Although no one program can meet the needs of all adolescent readers, the opportunity for teachers in all content areas to present a series of different, effective strategies can help students improve their reading. In a report from *Reading Next: A Vision for Action and Research in Middle and High School Literacy* (2004), Biancarosa and Snow recommend principals and teachers deal with the diverse literacy needs of young adult readers in a seven-step program that includes the following strategies:

1. **Develop** a school-wide literacy focus.
2. **Adopt** research-based instructional strategies.
3. **Offer** intervention classes taught by literacy coaches for students with reading difficulties.
4. **Give** increased opportunities for students to choose books for pleasure reading during the school day.
5. **Use trade books** that present content textbooks' key facts and concepts in a more appealing and understandable style.
6. **Use both** formal and informal assessments.
7. **Emphasize** pre-reading, during reading, and after reading strategies.

All of these methods are important in helping young adults learn to read for meaning. In addition, offering background information and interesting vocabulary strategies helps students become successful readers.

When Paula began teaching U.S. History and World History to high school students with learning disabilities and Dianne was a reading specialist, they followed the framework you are going to learn. This framework is a reading-based instructional program that provides the support students need in order to tackle required subjects that do not always interest them. Can you imagine what it would have been like for these students if Paula and Dianne had followed the traditional practice of just assigning sections in a textbook, having students respond to chapter review questions, and lecturing before giving a chapter or unit test? Pretty boring and tedious, right? Instead, students were taught how to be actively engaged in their own learning—how to think about what they already knew and about what they would have to learn in order to be successful. They learned to share their own ideas and opinions on topics and how to respond to necessary tests and quizzes. While performing these strategies, they *learned how to learn*—and isn't that really our job as teachers? None of Paula's students were going to become historians themselves, nor were Dianne's students at that time going to be writers or English teachers. Yet, for the rest of their lives they would have to know how to read and learn from their reading. Having students become life-long readers and learners has always been our goal.

Jim Trelease (2006) quoted education writer Alfie Kohn in his book *The Read Aloud Handbook*.

> Before a teacher, especially a middle school, high school or college instructor sits down to plan a course or thinks about evaluation he or she should ask the question 'What can I reasonably expect that students will retain from this course after a decade?' I know that if I'd been asked that question when I was teaching in high school and college, I would have found it profoundly unsettling, because I knew well, or would have known if I had been brave enough to face the question head-on, that all they would have left was a fact here, a stray theory there, a disconnected assumption or passage from a book. That should lead us to ask what it is we're doing. We sometimes end up making elaborate snow sculptures on the last day of winter (p. 59).

(Carol Jago, "An interview with Alfie Kohn," California English, Winter 1995.)

Think about what you actually want to accomplish as a teacher. Do you just want to provide the required information about a certain topic for students to memorize for a particular quiz or test—and then forget? If that is your goal, it's possible that a computer-based software program could accomplish your job. Students can listen to a lecture, read the text, and then be tested. However, if you would rather *teach* students how to be successful learners, to learn how to think about, question, and discuss important issues, then read on.

WHAT GOOD TEACHERS DO

Teaching is more than just the transfer of your fund of information on a particular topic to another person. Teaching involves transferring your enthusiasm and energy about your topic to your students. It involves showing others *how* to learn about what interests them, which then stimulates their desire to learn even more. How do you read and find information in a math or science text? How is that reading different from reading a social studies text or a novel? How do you find information in other media? Good teachers support their students in learning these skills. Expert teachers are those who truly understand the reading process and are able to respond to each student's personal needs as a learner. (Keene & Zimmermann, 2007, p.22-23)

WHAT GOOD READERS DO

Good readers are actively engaged in what they're reading: at least, they are most of the time. They know how to think about what they read and make sense of it. They can organize the information for future use, such as taking a test or writing a paper. As teachers, we tend to assume that all students can accomplish these learning skills if they just put their minds to it. Because we taught ourselves to be good readers, we believe everyone can do it automatically. Unfortunately, many students do not know how to begin to use these skills. They are not automatically good readers and because of this deficiency, they do not like to read, which automatically means, they don't.

The following are some of the reading skills we know good readers need to have. As you read over these skills, assess yourself as a reader. Do you:

Monitor Your Comprehension

As you read, do you keep track of your own learning and know when you begin to have trouble making sense out of what you are reading? Do you know what to do when you start to have problems understanding what you're reading?

Make Connections

As you read, are you thinking about how the new information relates to your own life, to other information you've already read in other books, or to your knowledge about the world events?

Visualize

Are you able to make a picture in your mind about what you are reading to support your understanding of the information? Are you aware of the techniques that authors use to assist you?

Infer

Inferring means understanding beyond what is stated literally in the text. It involves putting informational clues together, using your own background information, and filling in the blanks. If your friend looks outside and tells you that you will probably need to bring your umbrella, you can infer that it looks like rain. As you read you are expected to make a lot of inferences. Everything is not explicitly stated. Can you find instances when you have used this skill to good advantage?

Ask Questions

Do you have your own questions before you begin to read about a topic? As you read, do new questions pop into your mind? Do even more questions come to you after you've finished reading? All too often, students have become accustomed to questions coming only from their teacher. But good readers use their own questions to help them stay focused and interested in whatever it is they're reading about.

Decide What is Important

Remember the assignments where you had to find the main idea? Sometimes it was difficult, right? Perhaps every sentence in the paragraph seemed like the main idea. Good readers need to analyze and evaluate the information as they read. What is the author trying to tell us? Deciding what is important often depends upon your purpose in reading and being able to differentiate between what you think the author says is important and what is important to you.

Summarize & Synthesize Information

This skill pulls all the others together. It involves being able to think about what you learned from what you read. What new understanding was gained? In essence, what's the bottom line?

Good readers use these reading skills automatically. As you read about them, you might have thought, "Oh, I do that. I just never thought about it before." Good readers are what we call 'metacognitive'. That means they think about their own thinking and learning. But metacognitive skills require two important components: awareness and regulation. How many times have you read something, stopped, and thought, *I don't get that*? You're being metacognitive. You are aware of your own comprehension and whether or not you really understand what you're reading. The regulation comes in when you go back, read again, and use your thinking strategies to figure out what the passage is all about.

When common reading strategies are used in different subject areas, students begin to realize their curriculum is integrated. They can use similar reading strategies for the various types of literacies they are reading, whether it be a newspaper article, an internet article, an article from a library data base, or a fiction or nonfiction trade book. Unfortunately, secondary content area teachers may think the task of teaching reading and writing is the job of the English teachers and may say they don't have the time to teach these skills. Ironically, English teachers have just as much specific content to teach as other areas and do not have any more time than other content-area teachers do to teach students how to read to learn (Irvin, Buehl, & Klemp, 2003).

EVIDENCE & ACCOUNTABILITY

Evidence and accountability have become important terms in today's world. School districts are concerned with state assessments and evidence of student progress for purposes of state and federal funding. We look at this area in a somewhat different way. Assessment should be much more than a school-wide standardized test given in the spring of the school year. Assessment needs to be an on-going, daily gathering of information in each classroom to inform *you*, the teacher, about how well your students comprehend the information you are presenting. We believe you need to collect both quantitative and qualitative data. What's that? Quantitative data refers to numbers: quiz and test scores, percentiles, or reading scores. For example, look at **Figure 1** below. This graph presents a sample of the reading scores of a group of students in a high school English class. The grade equivalents and NCE (Normal Curve Equivalents) scores are ways to look at possible gains or losses across a period of time. You can see that C.B. made progress while A.E. did not. This finding represents quantitative data. Qualitative data refers to your observations as a teacher about each individual student's responses, writing, attention, and use of strategies. **Figure 2**, which measures qualitative data, gives more information about C.B. and A.E. that helps to interpret the quantitative data gathered. Both types of information are important in helping you plan how to teach. Based on the data, we know that C.B. is benefitting from the current instruction. However, A.E. is not, and it is our job, as teachers to figure out why and what to do about it. We use the term *'Authentic Assessment'* to differentiate between these types of evaluations and standardized tests. When we were in the classroom, we kept portfolios for each of our students. Inside our grade books were quizzes and test scores. Inside the students' portfolio were samples of daily work, dated

Name of Student		Grade	Sex	Fall G.E.*	Spring G.E.*	Fall NCE***	Spring NCE***
C.B.		10	f	5.7	12.7	20	56
C.D.		10	f	4.5	6.4	10	26
R.D.		10	m	5.4	8.3	19	39
A.E.		10	m	8.8	9.6	44	45
E.H.		10	m	PHS**	PHS**	58	71

Figure 1: Sample of Reading Reports: World History/Reading in the Content Area. 2002-2003 School Year

G.E.: Grade Equivalents; **PHS**: Post High School

NCE: Normal Curve Equivalents: NCEs are based on percentile ranks but have been transformed statistically into a scale of equal units of reading achievement. As a rough guide, if a student's total score is less than 4 NCEs above or below the score from the year before, there is at least a 15% chance that the student's relative achievement is not actually changed. If less than 11 NCEs, there is a 5% chance.

Student	Observations (Jan. 2003)
C.B.	On time to class; participated well in small group work using discussion web. Was able to determine key points in searching for different points of view and could then support opinion on topic. Wrote a strong paragraph in response.
A.E.	Late for class; had difficulty participating and staying on-task; was unable to complete the reading required for the task and did not participate in the discussion with group members.

Figure 2: Observational Notes/Students in Class

observations made by us about how well the student was doing when practicing a particular strategy, and samples of student writing and thinking about the topic. This type of data gave us a much clearer picture about each student than just scores from tests, and it helped us in planning future instruction.

DEALING WITH MOTIVATION

Isn't it sad that many students say that they don't like school? Why do you suppose that is? We can only suspect that it's our fault as educators. When students begin kindergarten, they tend to be excited about school. For many, that excitement gets lost, often as early as the fourth grade. Paula worked in both elementary and high school settings with special education students. Dianne worked with elementary and secondary students in Reading, English, and Language Arts and was a Reading Specialist for K-6th graders, most of whom had special needs. The lack of motivation for these students was a major concern for both of us. But we found the same thing to be true for many of the other regular education students as well. The tedium of listening, reading, responding to teacher-made questions, and then taking a test on subject matter that was considered to be uninteresting and boring was the undoing of many a student. In addition to typical types of reading difficulties students experience in areas of decoding, fluency and comprehension, an additional group of students are alliterate. This term means they can read but prefer to do other things, such as play sports, talk on their cell phones, or socialize with their friends and say they are just "too busy" to read. We knew we had to find ways to help our students.

Both Dianne and Paula became excited when they were first introduced to the basic ideas of content area reading instruction. Here was a way for Paula to make learning about history more relevant to her students' own lives and a way to support their learning throughout each lesson. Dianne could do the same with her high school English and middle school language arts students as well as her reading students in K-6 who needed her help with many different subject areas. Each day, students would become actively engaged in large and small group discussions. The students would learn how to ask their own questions about a topic and then work to find the answers to those questions. They would respond to the information in different ways. As you read on in this text, you will learn about this type of lesson structure and will read about ideas for activities that will support your students' learning in whatever content area you teach.

LESSON PLAN GUIDE/UNIT PLAN GUIDE

The framework for a content area lesson that is structured to support the reading needs is basic. It consists of 3 stages: 1) *Before Reading*, 2) *During Reading*, 3) *After Reading*. As the classroom teacher, you can follow this framework easily by asking yourself the following questions:

BEFORE READING

- What can I do to prepare my students for the lesson?
- What vocabulary/concepts might prove too challenging for them?
- How can I lead students to ask important questions and make connections about the information before we even begin?

DURING READING

- In what ways can I support my students as we read and learn about the topic?
- In what ways can I stimulate deeper discussions about the topic among the students?
- How can I help students monitor their comprehension, make important connections, infer, question, visualize, and determine importance as we read about and study the topic?

AFTER READING

- In what ways can I help students to synthesize the information that was presented?
- In what ways can I assess student understanding?

SUMMARY

This chapter examined the rationale for reading instruction in content areas. It discussed what good teachers do as well as what good readers do. In addition, the importance of ongoing, daily assessments was presented as a means of collecting both quantitative and qualitative data in order to inform teachers about individual students. The framework for a content area lesson was outlined.

REFERENCES

Allington, R.L. (2002). *Big brother and the national reading curriculum: How ideology trumped evidence.* Portsmouth, NH: Heinemann.

Biancarosa, G & Snow, C.E. (2006). *Reading next: A vision for action and research in middle and high school literacy.* Washington, DC: Alliance for Excellent Education.

Darwin, M. & Fleischman. S. (April 2005). Fostering adolescent literacy. *Educational Leadership, 62*(7), 85-87.

Irvin, J., Buehl, D., & Klemp, R. (2003). *Reading and the high school student: Strategies to enhance literacy.* New York, NY: Pearson.

Keene, E. & Zimmermann, S. (2007). *Mosaic of thought, (2nd ed.): The power of comprehension strategy instruction.* Portsmouth, New Hampshire: Heinemann.

Schoenbach, R., [et al]. (1999). *Reading for understanding: A guide to improving reading in middle and high school classrooms.* San Francisco: Josey Bass.

Trelease, J. (2006). *The read-aloud handbook.* New York, NY: Penguin Books.

INSTRUCTIONAL FRAMEWORK
BEFORE READING, DURING READING, AFTER READING

Research shows us that comprehension is based on three major areas:

1) understanding of the vocabulary and complex sentence structures found in texts;

2) adequate schema, or background knowledge, to support new learning; and

3) metacognitive skills: the ability to think about one's own thinking and learning (Westby, 2005).

The following three chapters will provide additional information about these areas and what content area teachers can do to help *all* learners in their classrooms to actually read content materials and learn and remember content information.

Teaching content information, as stressed before, is much more than just standing and lecturing to impart information. Paulo Freire (2000) describes students as "listening objects" (p. 71) when teachers practice the art of 'assign and tell'. This instruction refers to the long-standing habit of assigning a chapter to be read in the relevant text and then following up the next day with a lecture on the same information. To us, it is the likely cause of students disliking school and being disengaged from learning. Excellent teachers, however, engage students and work to ensure that they are actually learning. The before, during, and after reading activities described in the following chapters are appropriate for all levels of readers and will especially aid those who struggle because English is not their first language or because of learning difficulties. These strategies allow for differentiation and ongoing assessment of student progress.

We have selected, from a vast fund of choices, the ones which we have used and liked the best in our own teaching. Many more can be easily accessed on internet searches. Even after thirty plus years of teaching, both Dianne and Paula continue to find new ideas for ways to scaffold instruction by following the **Before-During-After** framework. Read on, and as you do, think about which ideas will work best within your own content area.

CHAPTER TWO
BEFORE READING

What do you do before going to a movie or watching a television show? Watch the preview? Read a synopsis of the story/plot? Check out who the actors are? All of these actions help you to be prepared to enjoy the experience. They increase your understanding and help you to decide whether or not you want to invest the time on the movie or television show. Have you ever gone to a movie and not had a clue about what it was going to be about? If that was the case, was it difficult to understand the plot at first? The same is true for most activities in life. As a potential participant, you have more success overall if at first you have some idea about what it is you are going to encounter, which is why it is beneficial to you to do some background 'research'.

These basic principles apply to reading and learning as well. Being prepared prior to actually reading the text helps improve understanding and enjoyment.

This concept relates back to what we know about the importance of activating schema. In 1977, R. C. Anderson developed the idea of *Schema Theory*. This theory states that prior knowledge is critical in order for comprehension of new information to occur. As teachers, we need to either remind students about what they already know about a topic or provide the background knowledge they need in order to learn.

How do excellent teachers prepare students for reading? The following will present some basic ideas for what to do. We bet you can think of even more, and if you look online, you will find a wonderful fund of other great ideas.

Thinking/Discussion Point: Think about yourself as a reader. What do you do before you actually begin reading a novel, magazine, or text?

KNOW THE TEXT

As a reader *you* know the difference between the different genres of reading materials, but are you sure that your students know about this variety of categories? There is a big difference between narrative and expository texts which will be discussed further in Chapter 7. Understanding these differences helps readers to know what to expect before even beginning to read. Knowing about different genres within these broader categories also helps them know how to read the material, how to adjust their reading speed, and what methods to use that will help them to understand what they are reading.

Just as we find big differences between cookbooks/how-to manuals, magazines, novels, and informational texts, we also see big differences between Science, Social Studies, Math, and Language Arts textbooks. Examine the content area books that you have and think about those differences. How is each textbook organized? When you are not around, students can (and should) use their textbooks as a resource, but they can do this only if they understand how. Math texts, for example, provide a sequence of skills. In other words, Chapter Two often relies on skills learned in Chapter One. The beginning of each chapter provides an explanation of the math concept being taught. Next are examples of how to apply the concept. Finally, problems to solve independently are assigned.

Paula remembers a high school junior who told her, "We don't use the book in Geometry. The teacher just assigns problems from it for us to do as homework." Unfortunately, by the time he reached study hall, he had forgotten what he thought he understood while in class and consequently, he didn't remember how to do the assigned problems. He had no idea that the processes his teacher had described and practiced during class were repeated in the very chapter which contained his homework assignment. Not knowing how to use the textbook as a resource made him totally dependent upon the teacher. Paula pointed out to him that, because she knew how to use the textbook, she was able to remember what she had learned many, many years ago. This example offers a great life lesson:

If You Know How To Read,
You Can Always Succeed.

You will be helping your students if you begin each school year with a discussion concerning your content area textbook. Show your students how it is organized and discuss how to use it. The time spent doing this activity will pay off as students will be more self-sufficient and able to complete assignments involving whatever text you use.

Thinking/Discussion Point: Examine a textbook from your content area. What features are important to recognize? How is your text organized? What will your students need to know about how to succeed when assigned reading in your particular textbook?

SURVEY, SKIM AND SCAN.

In elementary grades teachers call it a *'Picture Walk'*. When Paula taught a high school social studies class, she called it *'Picture Prediction'*. Dianne still uses the surveying method when introducing any textbook to her classes. She has been surprised at the number of students in advanced programs who have never used this process before. The process in both involves looking at any titles, headings, and bold print as well as illustrations, graphs, and charts and the brief captions or descriptions written underneath. Then students are asked to make a prediction about what the reading will be about. This discussion can then lead directly into a discussion about what is already known about the topic. If you listen and watch carefully you'll begin to discover who has a lot of prior information on topic and who has little to none. A follow-up pre-assessment activity on the topic will provide the data you need to plan subsequent lessons and differentiate instruction.

Thinking/Discussion Point: Pick a section or chapter from a textbook in your content area. Conduct a 'picture prediction' lesson. Think aloud about what would be important to look at and think about for your students. Think about how your text might be different from texts used in other content areas. What do students need to know about different texts?

BUILD BACKGROUND KNOWLEDGE

Many different titles are used for the same basic activity—Prereading Plan (PreP—see **Figure 1**), Semantic Maps, Webbing, Brainstorming. They are essentially the same idea. The purpose is to get your students to begin to discuss what they already know about a topic. The emphasis here is for the *students* to do the talking and then explaining to show their thinking. During this process you will be able to record both accurate and inaccurate ideas and then address them. Looking at timelines, film clips, or photographs, reading an old news articles, watching an experiment, trying to solve a real-life problem—these are all ways to introduce a new topic, develop real interest, and structure a framework for learning more. Remember, students will become more engaged in learning if they are able to express their own ideas and find that these ideas are valued. Envision that type of environment in which you, the teacher, are the facilitator, helping students to explore and find answers to their questions as they discover new information and ideas.

> **Pre-reading Plan (PreP)**
>
> **Purpose:** To activate prior knowledge about a topic or introduce new vocabulary.
>
> **Procedure:**
>
> Write a key word or idea that represents the topic that will be discussed.
>
> Ask students to give you one word or short phrase that they think of when presented with the key word.
>
> Write these ideas around the key word as they are presented including those that are incorrect.
>
> Add your own key words that you feel are important to the topic.
>
> After words are listed, go back and ask the student who volunteered the word to explain why he/she thought of that word. Address misconceptions such as words that were incorrect. Also, explain why you added the words that you did.
>
> Now students are ready to read the text. After reading, go back and revisit to revise words as needed.
>
> Source: Langer, J. (1981). From theory to practice: A prereading plan. *Journal of Reading*, 25, 152-156.

Figure 1: Pre-reading Plan

GRAPHIC ORGANIZERS

Once again, many different names are used for the same principle: clustering, concept maps, webs, and trees. The idea is to identify the main idea or topic being addressed in class and to link supporting information to it before beginning the actual reading. In social studies, a time line is a great way to begin to prepare students. They need to have an idea of when the topic being studied occurred in reference to other events in history. In language arts, a story map helps to identify the concepts of literature that are important, such as the setting, characters, problem, events, and resolution. In math, an organizer that shows the steps required to solve a particular type of problem is useful. In science, a hypothesis chart might be used. The **KWL** term stands for *What You Know/What You Want to Know/What You Learned.* **KWHL** adds the additional column of *How You Will Find Out.* This term is one of the most commonly used graphic organizers in classrooms—perhaps even overused. However, it serves the purpose of helping students think about what they already know and what they need to find out. The basic idea is to help students organize their thinking and create a visual representation of this thinking. When they can organize in this way, students become active learners in the classroom. Many different types of graphic organizers are already available. (See **Figure 2**) A simple web-search will provide thousands of ideas.

Note: Graphic organizers can also be used during or after reading to assess student understanding

Story Map (*McLaughlin, M. & Allen, M. B., 2002*)

Title:

Setting

Characters

Problem

Events

Solution

Timeline: Civil War

- 1820: Missouri Compromise
- 1854: Kansas-Nebraska Act
- 1860: Lincoln Elected
- 1861: War begins
- 1863: Slaves freed
- April 9, 1865: Lee surrenders to Grant
- April 15, 1865: Lincoln dies

KWL (*Sippola, A.B., 1995*)

What I know	What I want to know	How I am going to find out	What I learned

Figure 2: Graphic Organizers

and will be discussed in more detail in subsequent chapters. When using them before reading, you are preparing your students for what they are going to be reading about. It serves as a 'map' of information that will be encountered and allows students to think about what they already might know about the topic.

PREVIEW VOCABULARY

Vocabulary is always an important issue, and a difficult one to address because there is so much to consider. Nagy (1988) cautions us that any word study must be *integrative*, consist of *meaningful use*, and provide for much *repetition*. Assigning a long list of words to know is not going to be useful. In fact, the worst type of instruction is to give students 15-20 words, tell them to look them up in a dictionary, then to write the definition and finally to write a sentence using that particular word. Often, the student uses the word incorrectly even though the use may match the definition. Unfortunately, the student doesn't really understand the word. The assignment was, in essence, just busy work and another reason to dislike school. What can teachers do about this problem?

One of the first steps involves being able to select which words to choose. Beck, et. al. (2002) categorized vocabulary words into three groups: Tier I, Tier II, and Tier III. The following information about these 'tiers' helps teachers to decide which words should be focused upon:

- **Tier I:** These are words which are commonly used every day such as *school, teacher, desk, clock,* and *homework*. These words don't need to be taught because they are familiar ones students already know.

- **Tier II:** These words are commonly found in books, and the words upon which instruction should focus. Words such as *abhor, cogitate*, and *visionary* fit into the Tier II category. These words are not commonly used in regular conversations with friends and family. They usually aren't heard on TV or on the radio or in music. They are used, however in books, and unless one reads, one is unfamiliar with their meanings, and the downward spiral of being a non-reader begins. The less one reads, the less one is exposed to the vocabulary found in texts and the less one understands when required to actually read in school.

- **Tier III:** These are the words that are particular and important to the content being taught: the words found in math, such as hypotenuse, algorithm, and ratio, or in science, words such as metamorphosis or photosynthesis. However, these words are defined within the text. Additional attention beyond discussion and knowledge that they must be learned is not necessary. Students will learn them through the process of learning about the content that contains them.

Thinking/Discussion Point: Look through your content area textbook. Which words fall into Tier III? Now look again and list those words that would qualify as Tier II. Think about why it would be important for students to know and understand these Tier II words.

WORD CONSCIOUSNESS

The second step involves following the advice of Graves (2000). This concept is to help students to develop what is known as *word consciousness*: an awareness of the importance of knowing what words mean and an interest in finding out about new words. Of course, this process is easier said than done, which is why we have offered several suggestions for how to begin.

♥♥♥

Knowledge Rating Charts (Blachowicz & Fisher, 1996): These charts are easy to use and immediately introduce the key words that students need to learn for a unit. To begin, create a chart like the one below.

Next enter the words in the left column that you know are important for your students to know. It's best to have no more than ten words at a time. Students just check the appropriate column to indicate their familiarity with the particular vocabulary word being presented. As with all of these activities, the important part is the group discussion that follows. During this time, working with others helps the students to remember the important features of each word as it is defined within the context of your content area. After the small groups are finished, the teacher can have a final large group discussion to make sure the words have been accurately defined and used.

Concept of Definition Map (Schwartz & Raphael, 1985): This activity provides an organizational map to help students remember the targeted

Vocabulary Word	Can Define It	Have Heard of It	No Idea

Knowledge Rating Chart

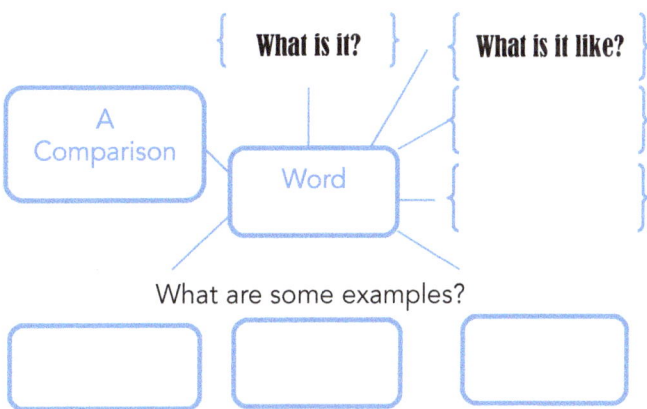

Figure 3: Concept of Definition Map

word. The word being defined is placed in a circle in the center. Around this word are different concepts that relate to it: Properties (what it is like); Category (What it is); Comparisons; and Examples.

Rivet (Cunningham, P., 1995): The purpose of this activity it to help students to think about what they already know about a topic. It also helps them to remember because part of the focus of your discussion is on the spelling and pronunciation of these key words. Begin with the following steps

- Choose 6-8 key words from the section/chapter that you would like your students to learn.
- Beginning with the first word, make a line for each of the letters in that word.
- Begin by filling in the letters, one by one, for that word, pausing to allow students to make educated predictions about what that word might be.
- If the students guess the entire word before it is fully spelled out, asked them to help you spell the rest of it.
- Follow the above steps for each of the words you have chosen.
- Make sure, as you present each word, that students understand what the word means and how to use it correctly in a sentence.
- When all the words have been presented, ask students to make predictions about what they will be reading and learning about.
- Keep the words posted on a topic board throughout your unit. Add new words as needed.
- As you are reading and teaching, point out those vocabulary words and continue to reinforce student learning and understanding.

Vocabulary Self-Collection (Haggard, 1986): Haggard introduced this strategy and we both have found it to be particularly useful when teaching to a large, diverse group of students. Sometimes teachers find it difficult to decide what words need additional focus because while some students know the word, others don't. This activity helps to solve this problem. Divide your class into small, collaborative groups. Each group is assigned to skim through a particular section or chapter that will be read and to select just one word that they predict will be important in the reading. They must present this word to the rest of the class, define it, and discuss why they predict its importance. Words that groups select should be posted and as students read, the predictions can be discussed and determined to be true or false. In addition, during reading, students can choose other words that they think are important to the content being discussed. They must always explain the meaning and explain why they think it is important.

Possible Sentences (Stahl, S. & Kapinus, B., 1991): After choosing 6-8 words that are important to your content, write them on the board in a list. Choose another 4-6 words from the text that you think are more familiar to your students and list those also. As a whole group, define the words allowing students to use what they already know. Following this introduction, have individuals or small groups create sentences using at least two of the words in each sentence. Students should then write these sentences on the board for the whole class to view. As reading progresses, definitions can be confirmed or revised as needed.

❦ ❦ ❦

Many more ideas can be described for vocabulary instruction. Do a web search, typing in 'vocabulary lessons'. When we did this exercise, the top of the list provided 200,000 teacher-reviewed lesson plans. Vocabulary development ideas are listed for every grade level and every content area. The important thing to remember is that vocabulary instruction needs to involve the following three rules:

1. Words selected for vocabulary instruction need to be integrated into other instruction throughout your unit.
2. Students should be guided into using the words in meaningful ways.
3. And, finally, word discussion should be repetitive—not just discussed one time—but rather discussion throughout the unit. (Nagy, 1998)

Words chosen for your lessons should be Tier II words—those that represent literate rather than everyday vocabulary. (Beck, et. al., 2002)

The over-arching goal of all vocabulary discussion is to develop *Word Awareness in* your students. Word Awareness means awareness of and an interest in novel words in general. Students who have this awareness notice words and are metacognitive about whether they understand word meanings or not. (Graves, 2000)

PROVIDE A PURPOSE FOR READING

All of us need a reason to read. In school it often boils down to the simple fact that a particular chapter must be read because it's the assignment and tests or quizzes will be given about the information. However, this reason is certainly not a strong one. Remember from your own days as a student and perhaps even today. Did you always read the assignment or did you wait and then try to cram everything into the last minute? Was it an enjoyable experience? Ideally, we'd like our students to read because they want to learn more about the subject. The KWL/KWHL helps in some ways because it sets a purpose for reading. Students read to find out answers to the questions they had in the *What I Want to Know* column of the chart. Some other activities that also help to achieve purpose are:

Predictions: Have students look over the material and predict what they think they will learn. Pretty simple, isn't it? However, one needs to go a little bit beyond just talk. Write these predictions down on a chart that can be revisited to confirm or refute. Students can check off their predictions as they read the text.

Anticipation Guides (Readence, J.E., Bean, T.W., & Baldwin, R., 2000)**:** See Figure 4 for an example of an Anticipation guide. To develop one, review your content material and write six to eight True/False (or Agree/Disagree) statements for students to read prior to actually reading the text. Students mark their answers first and the class can discuss and debate about the answers. Then students have a reason to read to check to see if they were correct or not.

Directions: Before you begin to read the assignment, read each statement below and then check whether you agree or disagree. Discuss your answers with a small group/partner. Then read the assignment to confirm your initial responses. After reading, go back and revise if necessary.

Agree	Disagree	
_____	_____	1. During reading activities only involve knowing how to outline or take notes while reading.
_____	_____	2. It is important to be able to find the main idea when reading the textbook.
_____	_____	3. Talking about the author's message is usually a waste of classroom time.
_____	_____	4. High school teachers should not have to be concerned with these reading strategies. Students should have learned them in grade school!

Figure 4: Anticipation Guide

Expectation Outlines (Spiegel, D. L., 1981): Expectation outlines are based on the sound premise that readers need to have their own questions in mind in order to provide a real purpose for reading. The outline is developed through a whole class discussion about what students expect to learn before reading a specific chapter or section of a text. These expectations are stated in the form of questions. Once enough questions are generated, students group the questions into categories and provide a label.

SUMMARY

This chapter has examined steps content area teachers need to consider before they delve into the actual material to be studied. We have discussed how important it is for your students to know how to use the textbooks from your class as resources for both finding and understanding information. We presented the importance of building 'schema' or background information before you begin and how graphic organizers can be used to help you build this background and prepare your students for reading. Of key importance, also, is the development of 'word consciousness': your students' awareness that it is necessary to know the meanings of new words in order to fully comprehend the materials that are encountered. Finally, setting a purpose for reading was described as a key component of successful instruction. Students need a purpose to read in order to keep focused and motivated to find out about a specific topic.

REFERENCES

Anderson, R. C. (1977). The notion of schemata and the educational enterprise. In R. C. Anderson, R. J. Spiro, and W. E. Montague (Eds.), *Schooling and the acquisition of knowledge.* Hillsdale, NJ: Erlbaum, 415–431.

Beck, I. L., McKeown, M. G., & Kucan, L. (2002). *Bringing words to life: Robust vocabulary instruction.* New York: Guilford.

Blachowicz, C. & Fisher, P. (1996). *Teaching vocabulary in all classrooms.* Columbus, OH: Merrill.

Cunningham, P. (1995). *Phonics they use.* New York: HarperCollins

Freire, P. (2000). *Pedagogy of the oppressed.* 30th anniversary edition. New York: Continuum International Publishing Group Inc. (original work published 1970).

Graves, M. F. (2000). A vocabulary program to complement and bolster a middle-grade comprehension program. In B. M. Taylor, M. F. Graves, & P. van den Broek (Eds.), *Reading for meaning: Fostering comprehension in the middle grades* (pp. 116-135). New York: Teachers College Press; Newark, DE: International Reading Association.

Haggard, M. R. (1986). The vocabulary self-collection strategy: Using student interest and world knowledge to enhance vocabulary growth. *Journal of Reading,* 29, 634-642.

Langer, J. (1981). From theory to practice: A prereading plan. *Journal of Reading,* 25, 152-156.

McLaughlin, M. & Allen, M. B. (2002). *Guided Comprehension: A Teaching Model for Grades 3-8.* Newark, DE: International Reading Association.

Nagy, W. (1988). *Teaching vocabulary to improve reading comprehension.* Delaware, NJ: International Reading Association.

Readence, J. E., Bean, T. W., & Baldwin, R. (2000). *Content area reading: An integrated approach* (7th ed.). Dubuque, IA: Kendall/Hunt.

Schwartz, R. & Raphael, T. (1985). Concept of definition: A key to improving student's vocabulary. *The Reading Teacher,* 39, 198-205.

Sippola, A.B. (1995). KWLS. *The Reading Teacher,* 48, 542-543.

Spiegel, D.L. (1981). Six alternatives to the directed reading activity. *Reading Teacher,* 34, 914-922.

Stahl, S. & Kapinus, B. (1991). Possible sentences: Predicting word meaning to teach content area vocabulary. The Reading Teacher, 45, 36-45.

Westby, Carol E. (2005). Assessing and remediating text comprehension problems. In Hugh W. Catts & Alan G. Kamhi (Eds.), *Language and reading disabilities* (2nd ed.) (pp. 157-232). BPSTPM. MA: Pearson.

CHAPTER THREE
DURING READING

After attending to all the steps discussed in the previous chapter about how to prepare your students before they even start to read, the next step in instruction is to provide support for your students *while* they are reading. When we examine our state's learning expectations for various content areas, we see the words *explain, compare, classify, describe, predict, interpret, identify, and evaluate* followed by specific content area jargon. This chapter about 'During Reading' strategies will help you to help your students be able to accomplish these tasks.

The list to the right is an outline of the topics discussed in this chapter.

During Reading

1. Dealing with Vocabulary
2. Reading Guides
3. Empty Outlines
4. Questioning
5. Collaboration Reading
6. Thinking Aloud
7. Formative Assessments

DEALING WITH VOCABULARY

As discussed in Chapter 2—*Before Reading*—dealing with content vocabulary is an on-going concern. The goal is to make your students highly aware of words and the need to know and understand their meanings. Teaching vocabulary is something teachers do throughout each unit of study. Before reading, we begin the process of developing this word awareness by introducing key terms that will be necessary to understand as students read. During reading, students should be encouraged to find other interesting, important words that can be discussed and used in class. Keeping a 'personal dictionary' handy is one good idea. Students can write words down in their book as they read, along with a brief definition. Another idea is to create a 'theme wall' where words are written in large print on colorful paper and posted on a blank wall in the classroom. See **Figures 1 & 2** for an example of each.

The important thing to remember is to take the time each day to discuss the words that are being written down by students. Ask them to share what they've added to their personal dictionaries. Add some words of your own. Make your theme wall one that students add to and discuss rather than one that you make on your own. Get your students involved and interested in the idea that words are interesting and fun to learn and think about.

Thinking/Discussion Point: Think about what you have done when you've encountered words with which you are unfamiliar. Is there a particular strategy that works well for you?

READING GUIDES
(Cunningham, P. & Shablak, S., 1975)

How often have you attempted to read a difficult assignment only to give up and plan to 'get it' later—or perhaps just plan to never really read it at all? An important skill that good readers use is the ability to 'monitor' their own comprehension. A good reader knows when the material is understood and when something in the text is confusing and difficult to understand. They also know what they can do to help themselves figure out what it is all about. That's the most important step, isn't it? These tasks of monitoring comprehension and figuring out what to do when you are not comprehending is, however, difficult for many readers, especially when they are trying to read something that is challenging and consists primarily of new information.

Good teachers understand this and make an effort to help their students 'get the picture'. Helping them doesn't mean giving a reading assignment one day and then telling all about what they read the next, however. That practice just leads to students deciding not to read the assignment. Helping your students means providing some structure that they can use while reading to help them grasp the difficult materials as they read the text.

Reading guides are a good way to provide the necessary 'scaffolding' to help readers find the important information—the main ideas and details that you, their teacher, think they should know. The reading guide is developed to lead the reader sequentially through the assigned text. It tells students what to focus on as they read and focuses attention on a

Figure 1: Theme wall in Language Arts Class

https://tse1.mm.bing.net/th?id=OIP.qWGP7FIckGgevuGIggPNDAHaE0&pid=15.1&P=0&w=246&h=161

Figure 2: Personal Dictionary

http://farm1.static.flickr.com/132/349693651_1d27ec5aae.jpg

> Read chapter one. As you read, use the following questions to guide your thinking and understanding about this material.

1. Skim over pages 1-3. When you get to page 4, stop and make note of what the author is saying about the theories concerning how children learn to speak. Create a chart below that summarizes this information for easy reference.

2. Read pages 7-8 about the components of language. What are they? In your own words, how would you define each?

3. Read on to the end of the chapter. List the 5 points that the author is asking you to remember as you read the rest of this book.

Figure 3: Reading Guide

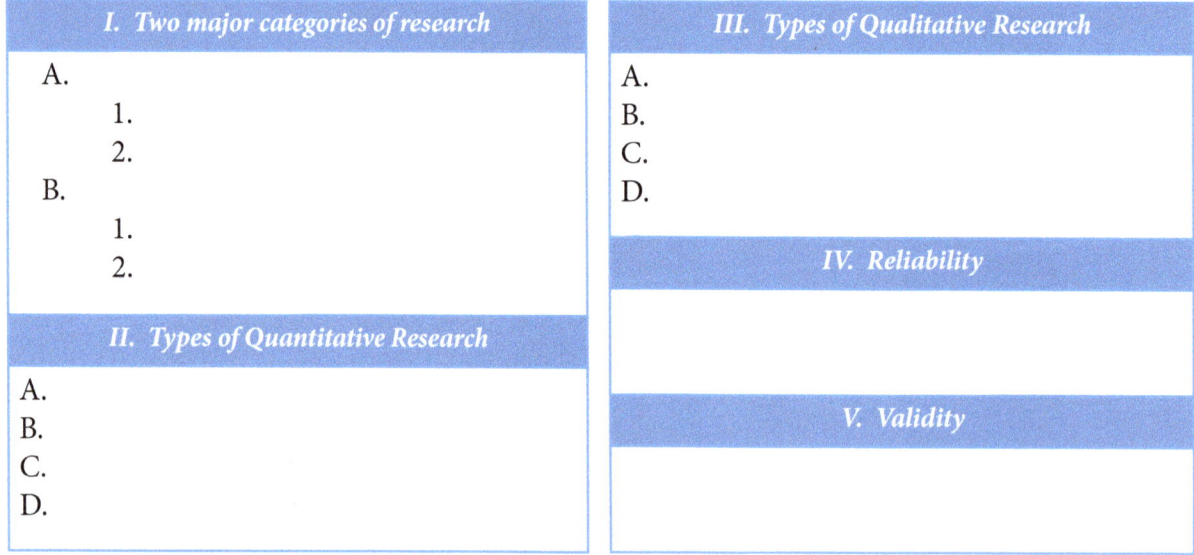

Figure 4: Empty Outline for Research Terminology

key point or asks a specific question for them to find the answer to. By using reading guides you are pointing them in the right direction in terms of helping them understand the difficult and new ideas being encountered in your reading assignment. See **Figure 3** for an example of a reading guide created for a college-level class on Child Language Development.

Thinking/Discussion Point: How could you use a reading guide in your content area?

EMPTY OUTLINES
(Hansell, T.S., 1978)

Empty outlines are related to reading guides. They consist of an outline form on which you have provided a very limited amount of key information and can be used for either a reading assignment or while taking notes in class. Rather than handing out PowerPoint notes for your students, ask them to listen carefully to the discussion and fill in the outline form as they do so. See **Figure 4** for an example.

These types of outlines can also be used as guides for students to use as they work to find information on an assigned topic. Both the textbook and Internet sources can be used.

The empty outline provides the needed framework for the student to use to help them find main ideas and details as well as to organize the information that they encounter.

QUESTIONING

Teaching students about questions is a very powerful tool to help them become successful learners. This doesn't mean having students read and then answer questions that come from the textbook or from the teacher. Just 'doing' doesn't always lead to understanding. Instead, students need explicit instruction about the types of questions there are and where to find the answers to those questions. Ciardello (1998), a high school English teacher, presented his research on this topic almost two decades ago. He categorized questions into four main groups: Memory, Convergent, Divergent, & Evaluative. The table below outlines some of the key information about these categories.

Students tend to do very well with memory questions. Those are the ones for which the answer is 'right there' on the page.

Memory questions also tend to be the type of questions that students are usually accustomed to answer. *When did the Civil War begin? What is the formula for finding the area of a triangle?*

Convergent and Divergent questions are a little more difficult. The reader must think and search for the correct answer. Some examples of convergent questions are: *How are reptiles and amphibians alike?* Or *How is reading instruction today different from reading instruction in the 1960s?* Some examples of divergent questions are: *Predict what reading instruction will be like fifty years from now.* Or *If government spending continues to escalate, how will the United States be affected in the next ten years?* These types of questions require higher level processing. The answers are in the text, but the reader needs to search for it, make connections and inferences, and decide what the essential ideas are as opposed to what is only interesting, but not as important.

Type of Questions	Key Words	Purpose
Memory	Who, When, Where, What	Name, define, identify give yes-no responses
Convergent	Why, How, In What Ways	Explain, State Relationships, Compare & Contrast
Divergent	Imagine, Suppose, Predict, If—then, how might….	Predicting, Hypothesizing, Inferring, Reconstructing
Evaluative	Defend, Judge, Justify, What is your opinion about…	Valuing, Judging, Defending or Justifying Choices

Figure 5: Question Categories

Evaluative questions ask for the reader's opinion. However, they require that the opinion be backed up by evidence from what was read and studied. For example, "*What is your opinion about global warming? Explain.*" Or "*Justify the succession of the southern states from the Union in 1860.*" The answers to these questions are based on your background information and your personal judgment. The support for your opinions needs to come from the text that is being read or outside research sources.

When students realize that there are different types of questions and that these differences influence where to find the answers as well as how to answer, it makes a big difference in many ways. Frustration is diminished. Test performance is enhanced. Understanding is achieved!

To teach them about these types of questions, first present the chart in **Figure 5**. Then have students categorize questions that you have written about a topic in your classroom. Help them to think about what type of information the question is asking for and then about where the answer to the question can be found. Next have students write their own questions. Remember, memory questions will be easy. Encourage questions from the other three categories. Practice talking about, writing, and thinking about the four types of questions. We can guarantee that your students will become better test-takers at the very least.

Thinking/Discussion Point: Using the information found in this text, think of one question from each category that could be asked in this class.

COLLABORATION/GROUP INVESTIGATIONS

Sometimes we like this idea the best because it involves the use of flexible groupings and collaboration, both components of effective classrooms. It is always important for students to be able to share ideas and discuss their opinions. All of us benefit when working with others to achieve a common goal. Hopefully, you are doing this very thing as you take this class. (Of course, effective discussions can only occur when everyone is actually reading and keeping up with the assignments, right?)

One of our most favorite group activities is called **Discussion Webs** (See **Figure 6,** Alvermann, 1991). Students form into small groups of 2-3 to discuss an evaluative-type question that relates to the overall theme of the lesson. This needs to be a question that allows both pro and con answers. Students search and evaluate information about the topic and find ways to support both sides of the question, much as one would in a debate.

Some such questions that teachers have used in Social Studies classes are: *Should the United States have dropped the Atomic Bomb on Japan*? Or *Should the United States have invaded Iraq*? These are controversial issues and there are two sides to the discussion. It is important for classroom teachers to present information on both sides of issues such as these. Students then read and research looking for the data that can provide support for the *pro* side of the issue as well as for data that supplies support for the *con* side. Once they have found the information they need, they meet within a slightly larger group and try to come to a consensus. Once that is accomplished, groups share their findings.

An example of this activity comes from a U.S. History classroom. A short article was found in the textbook about the development of the atomic bomb and the decision to use it against Japan. Both sides of the argument were presented in the article. Students were put to work, listing pros and cons for the use of the atomic bomb. After the factual information was organized, students paired up and shared what they had found. The next step was for them to meet within a larger group of 4 and attempt to come to an agreement about the answer to the question. When stating that 'yes' or 'no', America should or should not have dropped the bomb, students had to support their opinions with evidence from the text. As you might imagine, a very lively discussion and debate resulted from this activity. Some groups argued 'yes', some argued 'no', and one even admitted to not being able to come to a conclusion recognizing that it would have been a very difficult decision to have to make. What more could a classroom teacher ask for? Students are reading, evaluating information, discussing it with their peers, and being engaged throughout class—a dream come true!

A variation of Discussion Webs for math is to present a word problem. Students must then determine what information is essential to solving the problem and what information is extraneous. They

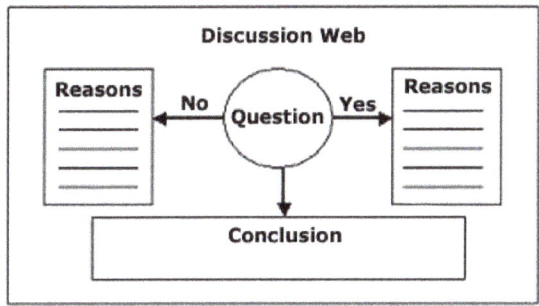

Figure 6: Discussion Web

scasscssap.org

then solve the problem and write up their conclusion.

There are many, many other group activities to choose from to use in your classroom. Students can form study teams to research content area materials of all types. Shared authoring can be used for students to report on their findings whether it be from a science-based application of the scientific method to research an important issue to solving a mathematical equation.

The important thing to remember is that students like the opportunity to share their ideas. Don't you as well? Listening is just one way to learn, and often it is not the best way. Think about a time when you really learned something important. Did you learn this in a classroom from a teacher's lecture or PowerPoint? Being able to explore, share ideas, and discuss information with other learners is a better way to engage students in real learning experiences. In addition, collaboration is a life-long skill that small businesses and corporations look for when hiring new employees. It's important for our students to learn these skills early on.

Thinking/Discussion Point: Think about your content area. What are some of the questions that you could use in a Discussion Web activity? List these questions. Now think of other collaborative activities that can be embedded into your classroom instruction. (If you need help, just type in Collaborative Activities for High School Classrooms in a Google Search.) Which of these ideas could you use in your content area? Discuss this with your partner or small group.

USING GRAPHIC ORGANIZERS

The graphic organizers you've look at prior to this are just a few of the many you can choose from to use in your classroom. Graphic organizers are simply a way to organize information and place it in a visual representation. When students create the graphic organizer themselves, it helps them both understand and remember the information. (Don't create it for them!) Social Studies classrooms can use Time Lines and Cause-Effect-Far-Reaching Effect models. Science and Math classes can use Problem-Solution, Main Idea-Details, or Steps-in-a–Process organizers. Language Arts Classrooms can use Story-Charts, Persuasion Maps, and Compare and Contrast Maps.

These are just a few suggestions. There are so many possibilities that it is impossible to name them all. The key is for you as the teacher to think about what it is that you want your students to learn. For example, in teaching reading, the teacher might want her students to focus on character perspectives. The graphic organizer would then look something like that found below.

Character in the Story	*Little Red Riding Hood*
Thoughts	Wants to visit her grandma
Feelings	Feels smarter than her mother
Actions Taken	Takes a short-cut through the woods

Character in the Story	The Wolf
Thoughts	He is hungry and is thinking about lunch
Feelings	He's a bully and feels like he can do whatever he wants
Actions Taken	He pretends to be a friend to Red and asks for directions in the woods

Character Perspective Chart

Thinking/Discussion Point: What graphic organizers would fit the best with your content material? How would you plan on introducing them?

THINKING ALOUD

As you can see, there are many different activities that can be used during the actual teaching of your content materials. These activities help to support readers as they read the content materials and attempt to learn content information. The most important thing to do, no matter what activity or activities you decide to use, is to explicitly teach your students about why they are doing this activity and how to do it successfully.

Look back at Chapter One. In the section entitled, 'What Good Readers Do', you see that good readers can monitor their comprehension, make connections, ask questions, visualize, infer, determine importance, and synthesize information. The problem is that many of your students will not be at that level of 'good reader'. An additional problem is that even fairly good readers will experience problems with the difficult texts and materials they encounter at middle and secondary levels. Your job, as their teacher, is to help them achieve both knowledge of content information and the skills needed in reading to attain that knowledge.

We know that good teachers always take the time to explain what students are going to be doing. This explanation is done within the framework of how it will help the students learn the content materials. Good teachers also need to take the time to carefully model just exactly how to do the activity successfully. The best way to do this is to practice the strategy called 'thinking aloud'. Thinking aloud refers to saying what is in your brain as you go step-by-step through the activity. You need to talk about what you understand and what might be giving you difficulty. You need to mention some of the vocabulary that you think is difficult (aside from those words in bold print), some of the sentences that contain a lot of information, and some of the concepts that need to thought about carefully.

If you are teaching your students to do a Discussion Web, first model and work through a discussion web using other simpler reading materials. If you are asking your students to create a graphic organizer, first think aloud about the steps you take as you create a graphic organizer on a different topic. The time you take to do this is well worth it. There will be fewer questions and misunderstandings throughout the actual lesson itself.

One final example. A 9th grade student was assigned a reading journal in his English class. The class was reading *To Kill a Mockingbird*, and the teacher told students that he wanted them to keep a 2-column journal and that they were to write something for each chapter in the book. In the left column of the page, they were to put the page number and a brief excerpt from the text. In the right column, they were to write some kind of connection. Below is an example of what the student wrote for Chapter 1.

Text	My Connection
Jeb broke his arm	I broke my arm when I was little
The door slammed	My door slammed

This student wasn't trying to be 'cute'. The problem was that he didn't understand the assignment. The teacher had forgotten to explain the purpose of the assignment. How would it help the students to understand the book? They just thought of it as busy work. The teacher also forgot to model what types of information would be helpful to understand the book. What should they look for in the text? What types of connections should be made? The students didn't know what to look for or what to write. And perhaps the worst crime of all—the teacher didn't actually read what the students wrote. If he had, he would have caught the problem early on. He just marked his grade book on random checks that pages had been filled out by the students in his class. The students here learned that their opinions didn't really matter after all.

FORMATIVE ASSESSMENTS

The materials you collect during this stage of your instructional framework are considered formative assessments. The classroom work that students do are all artifacts that will help you, as their teacher, know if they are meeting the objectives for your lessons or not. Keep their work in a portfolio, date it, read it, and evaluate their understanding and progress in terms of your specific content objectives. This is your best evidence of student progress and is much more important than numbers of grades in your grade book. These are the materials that you can show parents when they want to know how their child is doing in class.

SUMMARY

This chapter has examined a few of the many activities teachers can use to support students in the 'during reading' phase of instruction. We have looked at the value of reading guides, empty outlines, graphic organizers, and collaborative activities. We have also discussed the importance of promoting on-going vocabulary awareness through the use of personal dictionaries and theme walls and the value of teaching our students about different question types and where to find answers in response to these differences. Finally, we have promoted the use of thinking aloud throughout the instructional process and the value of all of these activities as a collection of formative assessments.

REFERENCES

Alvermann, D. (1991). The discussion web: A graphic aid for learning across the curriculum. *The Reading Teacher*, 45, (2), 92-99.

Ciardiello, A, (1998). Did you ask a good question today? Alternative cognitive and metacognitive strategies. *Journal of Adolescent & Adult Literacy*, 42, (3), 210-219.

Cunningham, D. & Shablak, S. (1975). Selective Reading Guide-O-Rama: The content teacher's best friend. *Journal of Reading*, 18 (5), 380-382.

Hansell, T.S. (1978). Stepping up to outlining. *Journal of Reading*, 22, 248-252.

CHAPTER FOUR
AFTER READING

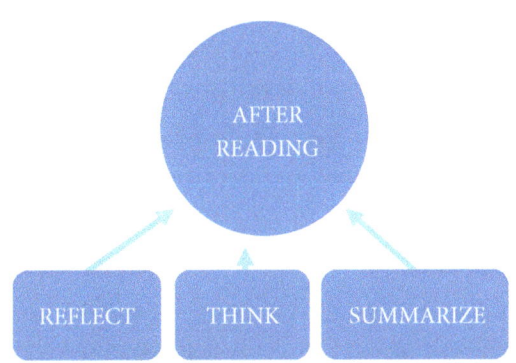

After reading, students need the time to reflect and synthesize the information that has been introduced. The following is a quote from Stephanie Harvey's and Anne Goudvis's book *Strategies That Work: Teaching Comprehension for Understanding and Engagement* (2007):

When we summarize information during reading, we pull out the most important information and put it in our own words to remember it. Each bit of information we encounter adds a piece to the construction of meaning. Our thinking evolves as we add information from the text. Synthesizing is a process akin to working a jigsaw puzzle. In the same way that we manipulate hundreds of puzzle pieces to form a new picture, students must arrange multiple fragments of information until they see a new pattern emerge. (McKenzie, 1996)

This chapter investigates a few of the many ways in which students can begin to accomplish the process of synthesis. To be able to be successful in this task, students need time to reflect about what they are reading and learning about in class. They need the chance to write about what you, their teacher, are teaching. Too often, when this step in learning is omitted, all those words both spoken and written, which you thought were important for your students to learn, become forgotten. Have you ever wondered how it could be possible for students not to remember what you just talked about the day before? As a student, were you guilty of letting classroom information go 'in one ear and out the other'? It is through written response that the learner can make the learning his or her own and remember it. By reflecting on what was read or taught, the learner actually learns. The following are just a few of the many, many activities that can be incorporated into your instruction to help your students learn.

EXIT SLIPS
(Fisher, D. & Frey, N., 2004)

Exit slips are an easy activity to embed into your instruction. As implied by their name, exits slips are used at the end of a lesson before your students leave class. Through their use you can rate how well students are really learning the key concepts being taught and whether they have any questions. Students can use index cards or just a single sheet of paper to respond to one or more questions about the material being studied or simply to summarize the topic addressed in class. Additionally, they can be used for students to ask their own questions, to solve a final equation in a math class, or to explain steps in a process. Decide what you would like to find out about your students' thinking. At the end of class, give students five minutes to respond to a prompt or specific question about what was discussed in class or read in a text. Collect student responses as they leave the room. The information you gather from this simple task is valuable in terms of both assessment of student learning and in lesson planning for the following day.

```
                                    Name
                                    Date
  Answer to exit question.
```

THE WRITING PROCESS
(California Bay Area Writing Project 1975, cited in Hairston, 1982).

It is primarily the task of language arts and English teachers to teach students about how to be good writers. However, writing, over-all, is the best way for students to pull information together and let you know what they have actually learned. The steps for the writing process are listed below. When writing in other content areas, students may also follow this process. Professional writers follow these steps as well. The more revisions made the better one's writing gets.

Other formulas may work for some types of writing, such as the 5-paragraph essay and "Power" Writing, but they do not work for all types, such as this process does.

Background: Brainstorming

Drafting: Putting first ideas in writing

Writing: Producing an idea with words

Revising: Reconsidering subject, form, and audience

Editing: Polishing simple mistakes and adding new ideas

Publishing: Producing a finished product

RAFT WRITING
(Santa, C. & Havens, L., 1995)

RAFT is a strategy that combines reading with a writing activity. Students read first and then demonstrate their understanding by creating a product of their choice. The letters are an acronym for: R=Role; A= Audience; F= Format; T=Topic. The flexible format of this activity allows students to decide what their role will be as they write, the audience for whom they are writing, the best form to use to demonstrate their understanding of the topic, and the specific sub-topic or focus of their work. The creativity embedded into this activity tends to be a motivator for creating the work itself. Students can demonstrate their understanding of whatever is being taught in a variety of ways as seen in the table below. This activity works in every content area and

Role	Audience	Format	Topic
• writer • artist • character • scientist • adventurer • inventor • juror • judge • historian • reporter • rebel • therapist • journalist	• self • peer group • government • parents • fictional character(s) • committee • jury • judge • activists • immortality • animals or objects	• Journal • editorial • brochure/ or booklet • interview • video • song lyric • cartoon • game • primary document • critique • biographical sketch • news article	• issue relevant to the text or time period • topic of personal interest or concern for the role or audience • topic related to an essential question

at any grade level where students are able to take a 'stand' or to explain an issue and write about it.

Raft Examples:

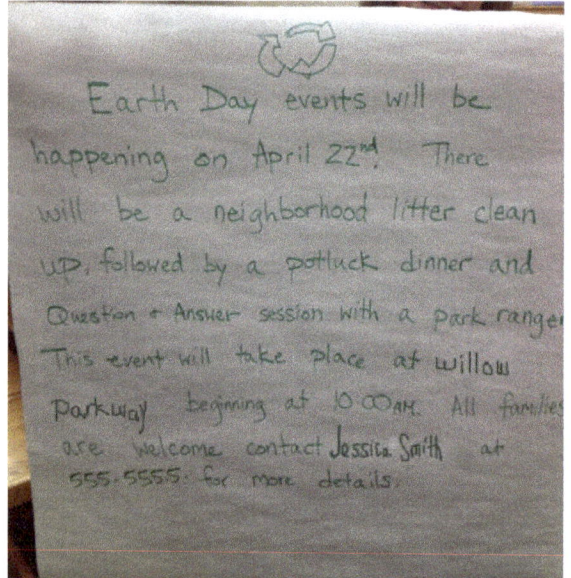

Role of a concerned citizen

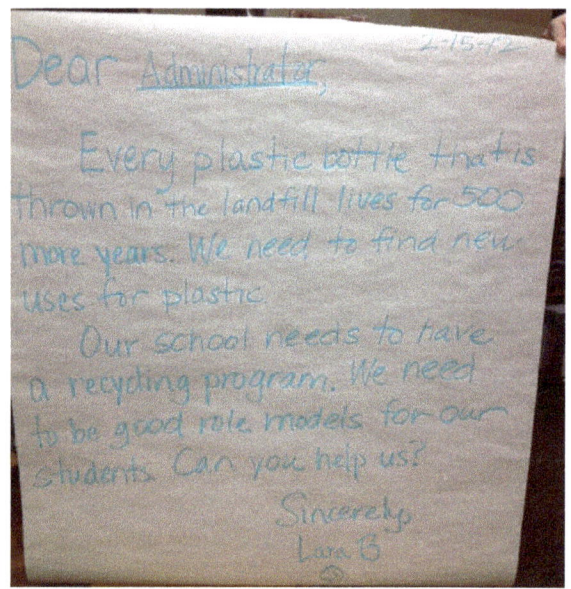

Role of Science Teacher

QUESTIONING THE AUTHOR
(Beck, I.L., McKeown, M. G., Hamilton, R.L., & Kucan, L., 1997)

This activity can be used during reading as well as after. Its purpose is to encourage your students to look for the underlying meaning in the text by examining the author's purpose and expertise in writing—then to develop questions that they would like the author(s) to answer. Beck et al. (1997) suggest that you follow the steps below to introduce this activity to your class.

1. Select a section of the text that you feel will generate a good discussion

2. Decide upon the best places within the text where you could stop and begin to think more deeply in order to better understand the message

3. Have students work together in small groups to create questions for each of those stopping places (Examples: What is the author trying to say? Why do you think the author used the following phrase? Does this make sense to you?)

As with all of these activities, of course, remember to first introduce the strategy by modeling for your students the types of questions that best help them to think more deeply about the material. Demonstrate how to think about different types of genre. When there are questions that go unanswered, discuss how to try to figure out a possible answer.

KWL
(Ogle, 1986)

The KWL strategy is a familiar tool used by teachers throughout elementary, middle, and secondary grades. It is introduced as three columns as seen below:

This strategy that can be used throughout the instructional plan with 'K' representing what students already know about a topic, 'W' representing what they want to know, and 'L' representing what was learned. Thus, a KWL is a good way to activate background knowledge, set a purpose for reading, and then summarize what, specifically, was learned. Many times that last step of thinking about and writing in the 'L' column is forgotten. Don't let that happen. Students need to learn that this entire sequence of thinking about text, represented by the three columns of the KWL, is part of the process of learning. At this point students can check to see if what they initially thought to be true, as represented by what was written in the 'K' column at the beginning of a unit of study, actually was true. If questions asked in the 'W' column were not answered, then students can determine what might be done to further investigate those questions. That final stage of summarization and synthesis to answer the question, "What did I Learn?" is as important as the first and second questions of "What do I Already Know?" and "What do I Want to Know?"

K
What I Already Know

W
What I Want to Know

L
What I Learned

RESPONSE WRITING
(Murray, D., 1984)

Response writing provides a format in which students can keep a permanent record of what they are thinking about and feeling as they read any type of text. Also known as journaling, this type of writing doesn't require a perfect, finished product. Students don't need to worry about making errors. They need only write to express their thoughts, make connections, develop questions, determine importance, and synthesize the information presented. Response writing is not the same as note-taking. It requires deeper thought than just writing down main ideas as they appear in the text. Again, learners will need you to think aloud about the process and to model what types of responses represent real thought and learning. At times, let your students know that their responses will be shared with the class. This practice often motivates students to do their best writing.

POETRY WRITING

Bio-poems (Abromitis, 1994): Bio Poems are a fun, creative way to have your students summarize what they have learned about a main character in a novel, a historical figure, or even an important scientist or mathematician. These poems follow a specific formula, making them easier to write than most poetry. They consist of only eleven lines. See the formula below followed by Dianne's example, written by one of her students:

(First Name)

(Four adjectives that describe the person)

Son or daughter of

(parents' names)

Lover of

(three different things that the person loves)

Who feels

(three different feeling and when or where they are felt)

Who gives

(three different things the person gives)

Who fears

(three different fears the person has)

Who would like to see

(three different things the person would like to see)

Who lives

(a brief description of where the person lives)

(Last Name)

The information within each set of parentheses should be filled in by the student as author. This strategy is a great way to synthesize the information learned and to add that personal interpretation that helps to stimulate motivation.

Dianne's Bio-Poem:

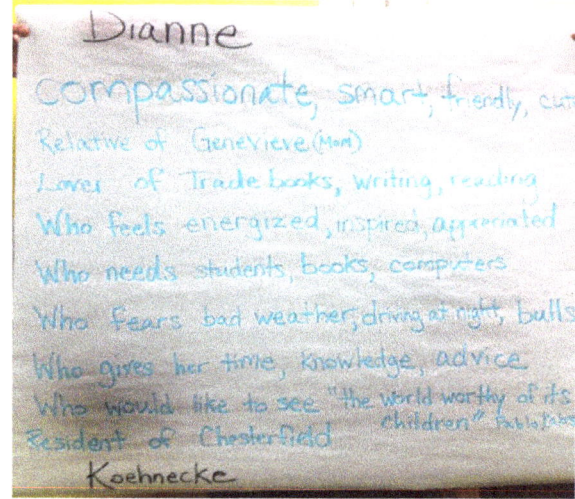

Acrostic Poems (Erithraean Sibyl, 12th century B.C.): Acrostic poems are another simple form of poetry that will engage students in summarizing what was learned about a particular topic. Simply list the letters of a key word down the left side of a

Puppy	Friends	T
Oodles of Love	Acceptance	W
Ornate	C	I
Dancing	E	T
	B	
Lots of Fun		T
	O	
Energetic		E
	O	
	K	R

page. Then go back and think of words related to that topic that begin with that letter. Look at the box below. We did Poodle. Can you fill in the rest of the blanks to create an acrostic poem?

Thinking/Discussion Point: These are very generic topics but consider how you could use this in Social Studies, Math, Science, Art, Music, a Foreign Language class or Language Arts. Practice with key terms from your own content area. Create an acrostic poem or bio-poem of your own.

Found Poems (Hobgood, 1998): Found poems focus on the important vocabulary and main ideas within a specific content area. The process teaches your students to think deeply about the message in an assigned reading. While reading, students should circle or highlight the strongest, most meaningful words in the passage. Instruct them to pay attention to the nouns, verbs, and adjectives that are the most important. These words are used to create a freestyle poem. Begin with a strong word or phrase. Follow the order of the words that have been selected, arranging them to show emphasis. Below is an example, using ideas from this very chapter.

> Summarizing—Synthesizing
>
> Constructing Meaning…
>
> What is Most Important?
>
> Reflecting…Creating Through:
>
> Exit Slips, RAFT, Question the Author, KWLs
>
> Response Writing, Bio Poems, Acrostics
>
> Deciding on Importance in order to REMEMBER!

MNEMONICS
(BELLEZA, 1993)

Mnemonic devices help students to organize and remember individual items such as names, facts, dates, a sequence of events, etc. They use both visual and verbal forms to categorize information and give it meaning. The first step is to identify areas in your content that can be grouped together. Then examine the first letter of each word and try to create another word or phrase using those letters. For example, a common mnemonic used to remember the Great Lakes is HOMES. This mnemonic is also an acronym because HOMES is a real word. The letters stand for the Great Lakes: Huron, Ontario, Michigan, Erie, and Superior. We actually remembered this mnemonic (acronym) from grade school and didn't need to look it up even now! Do you remember the Mnemonic for the names of the planets?

Thinking/Discussion Point: The ideas above are just a few of the many available for content area teachers to use in their classroom. Which ones do think will work best for your content area?

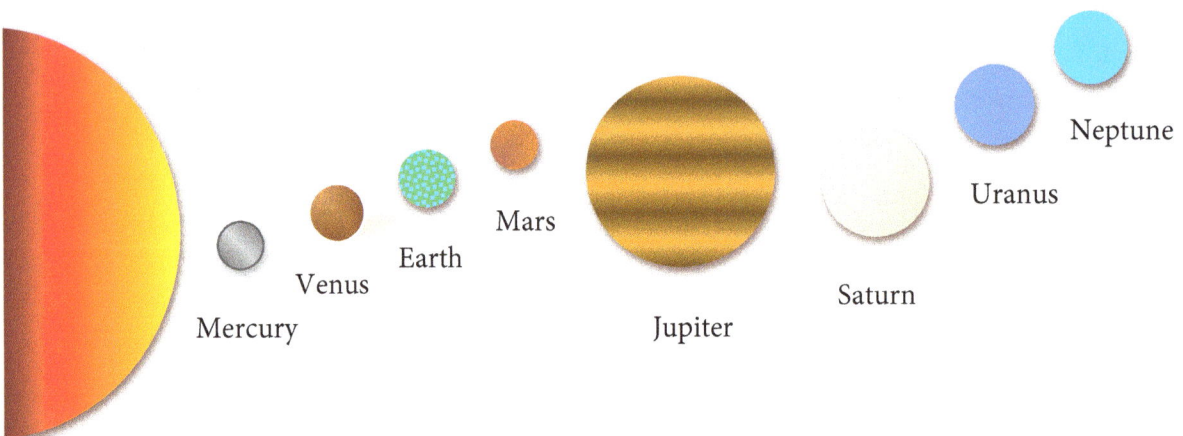

My Very Excellent Mother Just Served Us Noodles

SUMMARY

After reading, students need the time to reflect and synthesize the information that has been introduced. By reflecting on what was read or taught, the learner actually retains information. This chapter examined activities content area teachers can use at the conclusion of their unit to help students reflect upon what was learned and synthesize the information. These activities include exit slips, RAFT, Question the Author, the 'L' part of the KWL, Response Writing, different forms of poetry, and the use of mnemonics. When students reflect and produce a written response about this reflection, it helps them to remember what was learned—an essential step in teaching content.

REFERENCES

Abromitis, B.S. (1994). Bringing lives to life. Biographies in reading and the content areas. *Reading Today*, 11 (26) . June/July

Erithraean Sibyl, 12th century B.C—Acrostic Poems

Beck, I.L., McKeown, M. G., Hamilton, R.L., & Kucan, L. (1997). *Questioning the Author: An approach for enhancing student engagement with text*. Newark, DE: International Reading Association.

Belleza, F.S. (1983). Mnemonic-device instruction with adults. In M. Pressley & J.R. Levin (Eds.), *Cognitive strategy research: Psychological foundations*. New York: Springer-Verlag.

California Bay Area Writing Project (1975). Retrieved July 6, 2018, from https://bayareawritingproject.org/

Fisher, D. & Frey, N. (2004). *Improving Adolescent Literacy: Strategies at Work*. New Jersey: Pearson Prentice Hall.

Harvey, S. & Goudvis, A (2007). *Strategies That Work: Teaching Comprehension for Understanding and Engagement*. Portland, ME: Stenhouse.

Hobgood, J. M. (1998). Found poetry. *Voices from the Middle*, 5 (2), 30.

McKenzie, J. (1996). *Making Web Meaning*. Educational Leadership 54 (3). 30-32.

Murray, D. (1984). *Writing to Learn*. New York: Holt, Rinehart & Winston.

Ogle, D. (1986). K-W-L: A teaching model that develops active reading of expository text. *The Reading Teacher*, 39, 564-570.

Santa, C., & Havens, L. (1995). *Creating independence through student-owned strategies: Project CRISS*. Dubuque, IA: Kendall-Hunt.

CHAPTER FIVE
THE LANGUAGES OF DIFFERENT CONTENT AREAS: VOCABULARY

Every semester and every graduate session that we teach content area reading, whether or not it is face-to-face or online, we always have students complain that they really wanted to learn more about the vocabulary of their specific content area such as math or science or special education. Because every area has its own special vocabulary that students all need to know, we are including major terms from every subject area in this book. Students who major in these areas need to know terms specific to their content area well enough to teach them to students, who will then not only have an understanding of what these terms mean but be able to use them in that subject. If what they learn can be applied to real life situations, all the better. For that reason, Dianne and Paula have chosen major terms from every subject area that all of us will use throughout our lifetime.

Manzo, et al., offer concepts about vocabulary that most students probably do not know:

1. Only about 20% of an average adult's vocabulary (about 20,000 words) is learned through direct instruction. Reading, listening, and offering strategies that resemble the natural way words are learned is essential.

2. Noticing unfamiliar words is essential in building vocabulary, and this habit can be learned through effective strategies that incorporate not only teaching the words but practicing them in real-life

situations and acquiring them into one's permanent vocabulary.

3. A key component of vocabulary teaching is having students associate unfamiliar words with personal experiences and associations.

4. Understanding prefixes, suffixes, and root words (morphemes) can help vocabulary building.

5. Getting to a higher level of vocabulary development includes seeing and using new words in many different places and also knowing how to use context to obtain meaning.

6. Pre-teaching, or pre-reading difficult words before reading greatly improves comprehension.

7. An interest in learning new words is obtained mainly from observation and interactions. The teacher's interest in words and vocabulary can make a big difference in students' attitudes about the joy of language understanding.

(Manzo, et al., 2009, 149-150)

Strategies and activities for major content areas are listed below and in the following pages. Answers to some of the activities are found at the end of the chapter.

ENGLISH/LANGUAGE ARTS, SOCIAL STUDIES, MUSIC

ACTIVITY:

Read the lyrics to Bob Dylan's "With God on Our Side" (YouTube: 5/7/65 Bookleg Series) and listen to the song.

LESSON ONE

Find the wars in the lyrics and explain what happened in the wars.

Ex. Spanish American War.

The United States declared war on Spain on April 25, 1898. The war began when the Battleship Maine was sunk in the Havana Harbor on February 15 1898. The war ended on December 10, 1898 when the Treaty of Paris was signed by both parties. As a result Spain lost control of its overseas territories: Cuba, The Philippines, Guam, Puerto Rico and other small island near the Gulf of Mexico.

LESSON TWO

Literature Circles (Daniels, 2002). The following five roles are assigned to group members. Prior to beginning Literature Circles, be sure to explain how to do each of these roles and allow time for practice. For example, discuss what kinds of questions are relevant and useful to the discussion or what would make a passage meaningful.

- **Discussion Director:** Asks questions about the lyrics
- **Literary Illuminator:** selects meaningful passages/phrases from lyrics.

- **Vocabulary Finder:** selects interesting, unusual, or unknown words.
- **Connector:** compares lyrics with personal experiences, region, national or world issues and other literacies.
- **Illustrator:** Draws, provided picture or shows graphics that bring out meaning of the song.

LESSON THREE

Create a **Venn diagram** comparing and contrasting two versions of "With God on Our Side". Find the two versions listed below on YouTube.

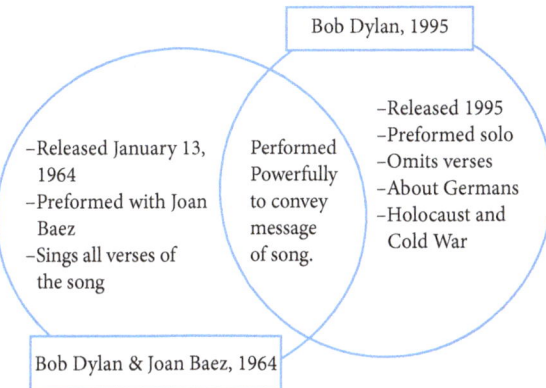

MATH

Advanced mathematics courses, such as trigonometry, have terms familiar only to those who have previously taken math courses which lead them to a point where the new jargon is understandable. Two useful websites for basic mathematical terms are:

http://www.mathsisfun.com/basic-math-definitions.html

http://www.amathsdictionaryforkids.com/dictionary.html

The words and definitions below are important because they are all practical terms for everyday life as well as mathematics. Each of these words can be used in a real-world situation.

Area: The number of square units needed to cover a surface

Average: The number found by dividing the sum of a set of numbers by the number of addends

Formula: A rule that is expressed with symbols Example: Formula for area of a rectangle: Area = length x width or A = l x w

Percent: The ratio of a number to 100

Variable: A letter or symbol that stands for one or more numbers.

Algorithm: A way of setting out a step-by-step mathematical procedure.

Mean: An average of a number of different amounts. Add up all the amounts and then divide by the number of amounts.

Median: The number in the middle of a chronological list of scores.

Mode: A score that occurs the most often.

CONTENT AREA READING

ACTIVITY

The Prophecy Square Game: match the terms to the definitions and then put the number beside the correct letter in the box. If numbers add up to the same sum across and down your prophecy is accurate!
(Answers at end of chapter)

A. Median	1. A letter or symbol that stands for one or more numbers.
B. Variable	2. A way of setting out a step-by-step mathematical procedure.
C. Formula	3. The number of square units needed to cover a surface
D. Are	4. An average of a number of different amounts. Add up all the amounts and then divide by the number of amounts.
E. Percent	5. The ratio of a number to 100
F. Average	6. A rule that is expressed with symbols Example: ____ for area of a rectangle: Area = length x width or A = l x w
G. Mean	7. The number found by dividing the sum of a set of numbers by the number of addends
H. Mode	8. The number in the middle of a chronological list of scores.
I. Algorithm	9. A score that occurs most often

A.	B.	C.
D.	E.	F.
G.	H.	I.

The Prophecy Square Game

ENGLISH LANGUAGE LEARNERS (ELL)

The following are terms that are associated with ELL students.

ELL: English Language Learners
ESL/ESOL: English as a Second Language now mainly referred to as TESL
TEFL: Teaching English as a Foreign Language (and EFL)
ALM: Audio-Lingual Method
CLT: Communicative Language Teaching
SLA: Second Language Acquisition
L1: First language
L2: Second language
Fossilization: a theory to describe when a language learner stops making progress in a second language
Interference: a theory to describe when a learner's L1 causes problems acquiring an L2
Interlanguage: a theory that L2 learners form a language somewhere between their L1 and L2 during the SLA process

ACTIVITY

Label objects in the room in second language and have students learn them (pictures: dog, door, things teens like)

Dog	*Cupcake*	*Computer*
Perro	*Pequeño Pastel*	*Ordenador*

| Clock | Cat | Refrigerator |
| Reloj- | Gato | Refrigerador |

FOREIGN LANGUAGES

When learning a foreign language, several major components exist: speaking the language, reading the language, and writing in the language. We asked a German teacher at our university to give us a few of the most common terms she teaches and we received the following list:

German vocabulary:

Nouns have the article 'der', 'die,'(dee), and 'das' according to word gender; 'die' for plural.

umlauted vowels = ä – eh , ö – oeh , and ü – ooeh.

The ß sounds like a double 's' – Straße = shtrasseh (street)

Numbers: 1 = eins, 2 = zwei, 3 = drei, 4 = vier, 5 = fünf, 6 = sechs, 7 = sieben, 8 = acht, 9 = neun, 10 = zehn; 100 = ein hundert, 1000 = ein tausend

Introductions and questions:

Ich heiße… (ikh heyseh)	My name is…
Mein Name ist… (meyn nameh isst)	My name is…
Wie heißen Sie? (vee heissen zee?)	what is your name?

Guten Tag! (gooten tag)	Hello, good day.
Wie geht's? (vee gehts)	How is it going?
Was kostet das? (vas kostet das)	What does that cost?
Ich möchte etwas essen. (ikh moekhte essen.)	I'd like to eat something.
Ich möchte etwas trinken.	I'd like to drink something
Können Sie mir sagen, wo ein Restaurant ist? (koehnnen zee mir zagen, vo eyn Restaurant isst?)	Can you please tell me, where a restaurant is?
Wo ist ein Hotel? (vo isst eyn Hotel?)	Where is the hotel?
Haben Sie ein Zimmer?	Do you have a room?
Bezahlen, bitte! (betsahlen bihtteh)	I'll pay now.
Wo ist das Klo? (vo ist das klo?)	Where is the toilet?
Auf Wiedersehen (aoof veederzehn)	Goodbye
Wo ist die Apotheke? (vo isst dee apotehke - pharmacy)	Where is the pharmacy?

Ich habe Sodbrennen (zodbrennn)	heartburn
Ich habe Kopfschmerzen (kopfshmertsen)	headache
Ich habe Magenschmerzen (mahgenshmertsen)	stomach pains

Der (Masculine)
Bus = Bus
Zug = Train
Die (Feminine)
Straße = Street
Shule = School
Das (Neuter)
Klo = Toilet
Restaurant = Restaurant

ACTIVITY

Translate a movie scene into German or whatever language you are studying and perform (*Examples: Mean Girls, Ferris Bueller's Day off, The Breakfast club*).

SPECIAL EDUCATION

Homogeneous grouping: An educational practice in which students of similar abilities are placed within the same instructional groups.

Referral: Notice to a school district, given by a teacher or other professional in the field, that a child may be in need of special education.

Inclusion: providing accommodations and supports to enable all students to receive an appropriate and meaningful education on the same setting, including participation in extracurricular and non-academic activities.

Modifications: Substantial changes in what the student is expected to demonstrate; includes changes in instructional level, content and performance criteria; may include changes in test form or format; includes alternative assignments.

Co-teaching: A program model in which the special education teacher demonstrates for or team teaches with the general classroom teacher to help a students with special needs be successful in a regular classroom.

Behavior Intervention Plan: The plan of action designed and implemented to address behavior that may negatively impact the success of a student with disabilities; plan includes positive strategies, program modifications, and aids and supports that address a student's disruptive behaviors and allows the child to be educated in the least restrictive environment.

Paraprofessional: A school employee who is assigned to assist students with special needs; paras usually work one-on-one or with a small group of students.

Present level of academic achievement and functional performance (Academic and Functional Performance): A statement on the IEP that describes what the child knows and can do at this time; includes how the child's disability affects the child's involvement and progress in the general education curriculum; or for preschool children, as appropriate and how the disability affects the child's participation in appropriate activities.

Since special education is not one specific content area, these vocabulary terms were chosen to provide special education vocabulary that will most likely appear in all classrooms which include students with special needs. It is important that all teachers, not just special education teachers, are familiar with these terms so that the highest levels of support can be provided for not only students with disabilities, but for every student in the classroom.

ACTIVITY:

Complete the Crossword Puzzle:

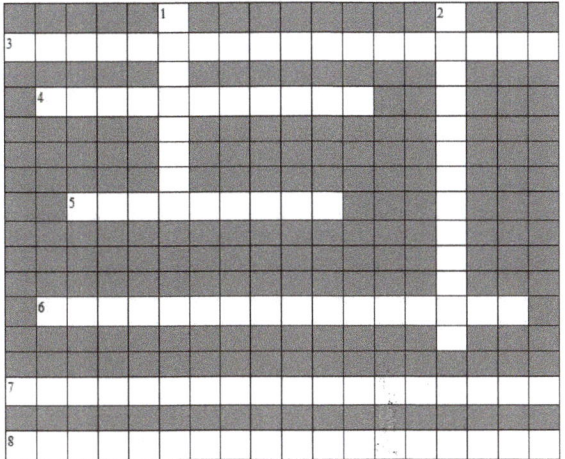

Across:

3. An educational practice in which students of similar abilities are placed within the same instructional groups.

4. A program model in which the special education teacher demonstrates for or team teaches with the general classroom teacher to help a students with special needs be successful in a regular classroom.

5. Providing accommodations and supports to enable all students to receive an appropriate and meaningful education on the same setting, including participation in extracurricular and non-academic activity

6. A school employee who is assigned to assist students with special needs; paras usually work one-on-one or with a small group of students.

7. The plan of action designed and implemented to address behavior that may negatively impact the success of a student with disabilities; plan includes positive strategies, program involves modifications

8. A statement on the IEP that describes what the child knows and can do at this time; includes how the child's disability affects the child's involvement and progress in the general education curriculum; or for preschool children, as appropriate and how the disability affects the child's participation in appropriate activities.

Down:

1. Notice to a school district, given by a teacher or other professional in the field, that a child may be in need of special education.

2. Substantial changes in what the student is expected to demonstrate; includes changes in instructional level, content and performance criteria; may include changes in test form or format; includes alt.

(*Answers at end of chapter.)

ART

Abstract Art: In abstract art, what is perceived as objective reality is simplified, or restructured to express the intrinsic, sometimes invisible qualities of the subject.

Baroque: A period in western art dating roughly from 1580-1700. As an adjective, baroque usually refers to art which is extravagant and dramatic, or which shows a highly elaborate integration of curvilinear and rectilinear form.

Classical: As an adjective, classical refers to art which utilizes ideals of Classical Art (i.e. Greek or Roman Art), OR which emphasizes the intellect, clarity and control.

Collage: The addition of several materials attached to a two dimensional surface.

Composition: The organization of the different "Elements of Art" into a inified whole.

Design: The plan or skeleton which serves as the foundation for the total work of art. In a more narrow sense it is the arrangement of shapes within a two dimensional surface.

Elements of Art: The fundamental graphic devices used by an artist in composing a work of art: color, line, shape, texture, and tone.

Hue: The technical name for a color, i.e. red, green, blue.

Intensity: The strength or purity of color.

Principles of Art: The organization of the "Elements of Art" through contrast, emphasis, balance, movement, repetition, rhythm, proportion, etc.

(Taken from: http://www.bookemon.com/read-book/136470)

ACTIVITY

Create an image (Drawing, collage, or digital image) that uses as many of the terms of above as possible.

Hue, Intensity, Composition, Collage, Classical, Elements of Art, Abstract Art, Composition, Principles of Art

SCIENCE

Earth Science: The branch of science dealing with the constitution of the earth and its atmosphere.

Geology: The science of the origin, history, and structure of the earth, and the physical, chemical, and biological changes that it has experienced or is experiencing.

Oceanography: The exploration and study of the ocean.

Paleontology: The science of the forms of life that existed in prehistoric or geologic periods.

Meteorology: The science that deals with the atmosphere and its phenomena, such as weather and climate.

Botany: The study of plants.

Zoology: The science that covers animals and animal life.

Physical Science: Any of the sciences concerned with nonliving matter, energy, and the physical properties of the universe.

Chemistry: The science that deals with the composition, properties reactions, and the structure of matter.

Astronomy: The study of the universe beyond the earth's atmosphere.

One science teacher chose to define the three main branches of science including examples of each branch. To familiarize her students with these terms, she divided her class into three groups. Each group would discuss one of the branches in depth. Next, she would have the groups share their findings including specific examples of each branch with the entire class.

ACTIVITY

The comedian, Rich Hall created sniglets during the 1980's. Sniglets can be used as a reading strategy to build morphemic understanding (Altieri, 2011). A morpheme just means the tiniest piece of meaning, such as a root word. We will give you a list of common morphemes used in Scientific words. Play sniglets: words not in the dictionary that should be, affix/suffix/prefix. Look at list, make up word, define your word, use your word in a sentence, draw a picture showing your word.

Cide (kill)	Ecto (outter)	Endo (within)
Meta- (Change)	Meter (measure)	ology (Study of)
Eu (well and good) phobia (fear)	Hyper (too much) Photo (light)	

Word	Definition
Macrobiliophon Macro=Large Biblio=Book Phon=Sound	A children's book with sound to read the book for you and give the pictures sound. Ex. Elmo books, Thomas the Choo choo train book

Sentence	Picture
'People don't really find a lot of macrobibliophons because they are not commonly in book stores. (Macrobiliophons are sometimes difficult to find.)	

Morpheme Examples

CONTENT AREA READING

USEFUL WEBSITES

https://www.teachingenglish.org.uk/article/vocabulary-activities

https://www.vocabulary.com/lists/137567

https://www.vocabulary.com/lists/558097

http://www.k12reader.com/effective-strategies-for-teaching-vocabulary/

SUMMARY

The emphasis in this chapter was in knowing and using major terms from different content areas. Highlights of major definitions for content areas were described, as well as strategies for how to best teach content vocabulary terms to students.

ANSWERS:

A. 8	B. 1	C. 6
D. 3	E. 5	F. 7
G. 4	H. 9	I. 2

Answers to The Prophecy Game

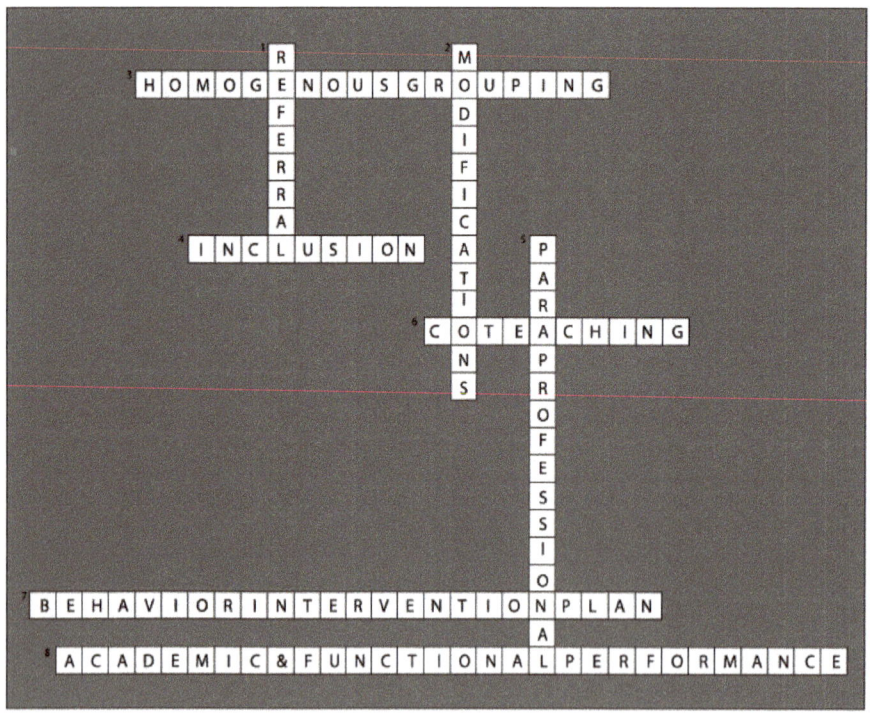

Answers to Special Education Crossword

REFERENCES

Altieri, J. (2011). Content counts: Developing disciplinary skills, K-6: Newark, DE: IRA

Chandler-Olcott, K., & Mahar, D. (2003). "Tech-savviness" meets multiliteracies: Exploring adolescent girls' technology-related literacy practices. *Reading Research Quarterly,* (38)1, 56-385.

Daniels, H. (2002). Literature circles: Voice and choice in book clubs and reading groups. Portsmouth, NH: Stenhouse.

Jones-Kavalier, B. R. & Flannigan, S.L. (2006). Connecting the digital dots: Literacy of the 21st century. *Education Quarterly* (29), 2.

Lieu, D. J. (2010). The future of reading: Misalignments of public policy, assessment, and instruction in an online world of new literacies, *School Library Journal's Leadershiip Summit 2010*: The Future of Reading.

Luke, A. (2007, May 31). Dr. Allan Luke: The New Literacies. In *Webcasts for Education.*

Manzo, U.C., Manzo, A.V., & Thomas, M.M. (2009) Content area literacy: A framework for reading-based instruction, 5th Ed. Hoboken, NJ: John Wiley & Sons, Inc.

Motoko, R. (n.d.). Literacy Debate: Online, R U Really Reading? in *The New York Times/Books*. RetrievedOctober2, 2011, from http://www.nytimes.com/2008/07/27/books/27reading.html

O'Brien, D. & Scharber, C. (2008, Sept.). Digital literacies go to school: Potholes and possibilities. *Journal of Adolescent and Adult Literacy (52)1*, 66-68.

http://americasbesthistory.com/abhtimeline1920.html

http://www.amathsdictionaryforkids.com/dictionary.html

https://www.theartofed.com/2018/03/22/the-most-creative-way-to-teach-your-students-art-vocabulary/

https://myvocabulary.com/word-list/math-vocabulary/

https://www.socialstudies.com

CHAPTER SIX
READABILITY LEVELS

Three major readability formulas used to find reading levels will be presented in this chapter. Checklists to help teachers determine the reliability of these formulas will also be introduced.

READING LEVELS:
INDEPENDENT, INSTRUCTIONAL, AND FRUSTRATION

Based on many years of teaching reading in the content area to both undergraduate and graduate students, Dianne and Paula have learned that teachers really want to understand the concept of readability and be able to use their knowledge to help students read well.

To help students understand the difficulty of the material they are reading, Dianne and Paula introduce students to the terms, Independent Level, Instructional Level, and Frustration Level. The Independent Level means that a student can read material with no help from the teacher with either word identification or comprehension. Reading at an Instructional Level indicates students can read the material, but they do need some help from the teacher with either identification of some of the words or with the ability to understand it. At the Frustration Level, the material is far too difficult for the students, even with teacher instruction. Once teachers understand how to apply these levels to each student, they become better instructors because they are able to assign the accurate levels of texts for individual readers.

Using readability formulas can help teachers determine the reading levels of the texts they use in their classrooms. Several readability formulas have been developed and are presented in the following pages.

LEXILE FORMULA

The **Lexile method** (www.lexile.com) is used by the majority of textbooks, but it involves a software program that must be ordered. It is widely used throughout the country. It is often used in tests that measure reading comprehension and includes scores that can determine what grade levels would be best suited for different material. The scores range from BR (Beginning Reader) to HL (High Level Reader). Your school districts may not be able to afford it, but it is used by major publishers, such as Scholastic. **READING ABILITY** is having the capacity to read and understand passages. The Lexile system calculates passage readability from just two areas: sentence length and word familiarity. Knowledge of words are obtained from John Carroll's sample of five million words in the 1971 *Word Frequency Book*. The Lexile reading ability is measured by finding out what Lexile passage readability a person can understand with 75 percent accuracy. Success means recognizing what words are needed to mend gaps inserted in passages or in other words, using a cloze method. (Stenner, 19812, 1983, 1987). The Lexile formula is based on two ideas:

1. Meaning: the more familiar the words, the easier the passage is to read; the more unfamiliar the words, the harder.

2. Structure: the shorter the sentences, the easier the passage is to read; the longer the sentences, the harder.

These ideas apply to whatever is read, apart from content. They apply whether we like what we are reading or not, whether it is prose, document, or quantitative. (1998, Wright, B.D. & Stenner, A.J.).

For individual teachers, other methods of measurement to determine readability can be useful, particularly if several different techniques are combined for reliability and validity.

Grade	Reader Measures (Interquartile Range, Mid-Year)	Text Measures (From the Lexile Map)
1	Up to 300L	200L to 400L
2	140L to 500L	300L to 500L
3	330L to 700L	500L to 700L
4	445L to 810L	650L to 850L
5	565L to 910L	750L to 950L
6	665L to 1000L	850L to 1050L
7	735L to 1065L	950l to 1075L
8	805L to 1100L	1000L to 1100L
9	855L to 1165L	1050L to 1150L
10	905L to 1195L	1100L to 1200L
11&12	940L to 1210L	1100L to 1300L

FRY FORMULA

Another, useful technique widely used is the Fry method, designed by Edward Fry, formerly of Rutgers University (http://kathyschrock.net/fry/fry.html). A sample of 300 words is required. The aver-

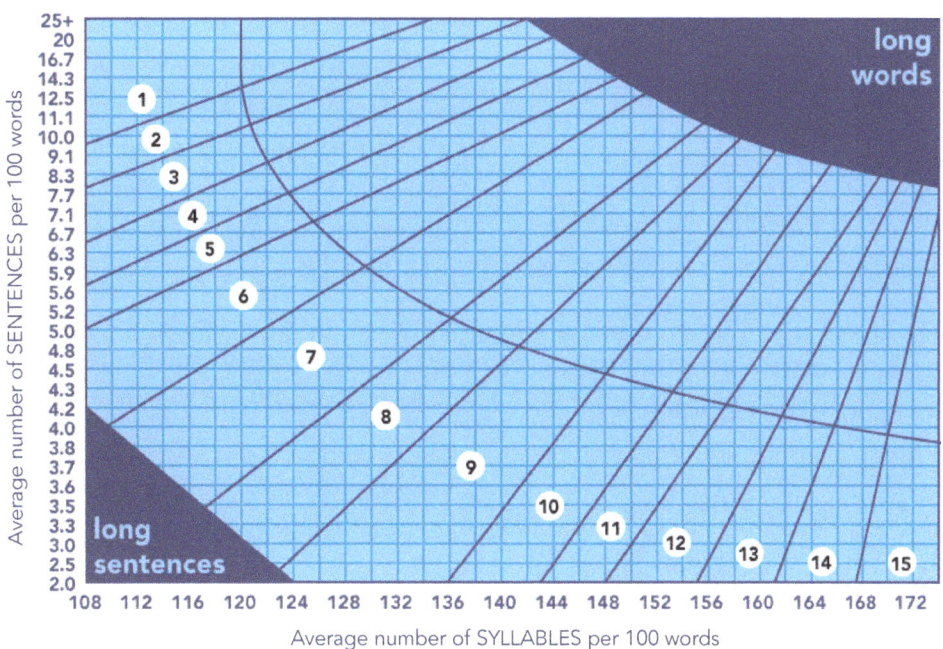

Fry, Edward. Elementary Reading Instruction. McGraw-Hill, 1977

age number of syllables and sentences in every 100 words plotted on the Fry graph can determine the grade level of specific material. It is better to take several samples from different sections of the reading material to make sure the result is accurate.

DIRECTIONS FOR USE OF THE FRY READABILITY GRAPH:

1. Select three 100-word passages from a book or an article. We recommend a beginning, middle, and ending paragraph, but your choices may be random.
2. Count the total number of syllables as well as the total number of sentences per 100 words. Then divide to get an average (mean).
3. Next, plot the average number of syllables and the average number of sentences per 100 words on the graph to determine the grade level of the material.
4. If you think your results are inconclusive, do additional paragraphs. The article, textbook, trade book, or online material may have uneven readability, which you can determine if you add more paragraphs for an average.
5. Little of the reading material will fall in the solid black area, but if it does, the grade level scores are not valid.

(Paraphrased and changed from original Kathy Schrock website, 1995. http://school.

discoveryeducation.com/schrockguide/fry/fry.html)

EXAMPLE:

This example comes from *Harry Potter and the Order of the Phoenix*. Three paragraphs were taken, one from the beginning, one from the middle, and one from the end. Each paragraph was 100 words long.

Paragraph One: Syllables: 136, Sentences: 9.5
Paragraph Two: Syllables: 147, Sentences: 9
Paragraph Three: Syllables: 146, Sentences: 13

This book is at a 6th grade reading level.

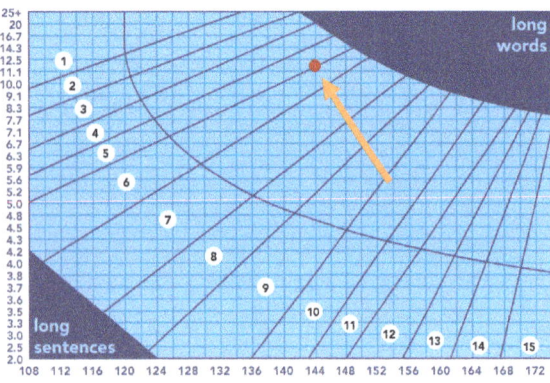

Average per 100 words:

Syllables: 143

Sentences: 10.5

THE FLESCH-KINKAID FORMULA

The easiest formula to determine readability level is the Flesch-Kinkaid**,** which is used by the US Government Department of Defense as a standard. This test was created by *Rudolf Flesch* in the 1940's and later enhanced by *John P. Kincaid*. In 1951, Farr, Jenkins, and Patterson simplified the formula further by changing the syllable count. It involves a specific formula that uses the average words within a sentence in a paragraph and the average syllables in the paragraph. In 1975, in a project sponsored by the military, the Reading Ease formula was recalculated to give a grade-level score. The revised formula was called the **Flesch–Kincaid Grade-Level** formula. The Flesch–Kincaid formula is one of the most popular and heavily tested formulas. It correlates 0.91 with comprehension as measured by reading tests. What is useful about this formula is that it is in all Microsoft Word versions, a common word processing software. Yearly versions of *Word* change the way to determine the formula, but by using the icons on the top of the program, it is easy to determine three important factors: the percent of passive sentences, the percentile of reading ease, and the grade level. The following example is given from Word 2015.

1. Once you have checked the "Show Readability Level" (see above), you will need to type in the passages or cut and paste them onto your page.

2. Next do a spell check.

3. When you finish checking your passage, the readability level will be shown. This short list of directions paragraph will be now be highlighted to show the results of the Flesh-Kinkaid Readability Level.

A good idea when choosing textbooks is to use at least two of the three different methods for better validity and reliability. If the teacher or student just wants a general idea of readability, then the Flesch-

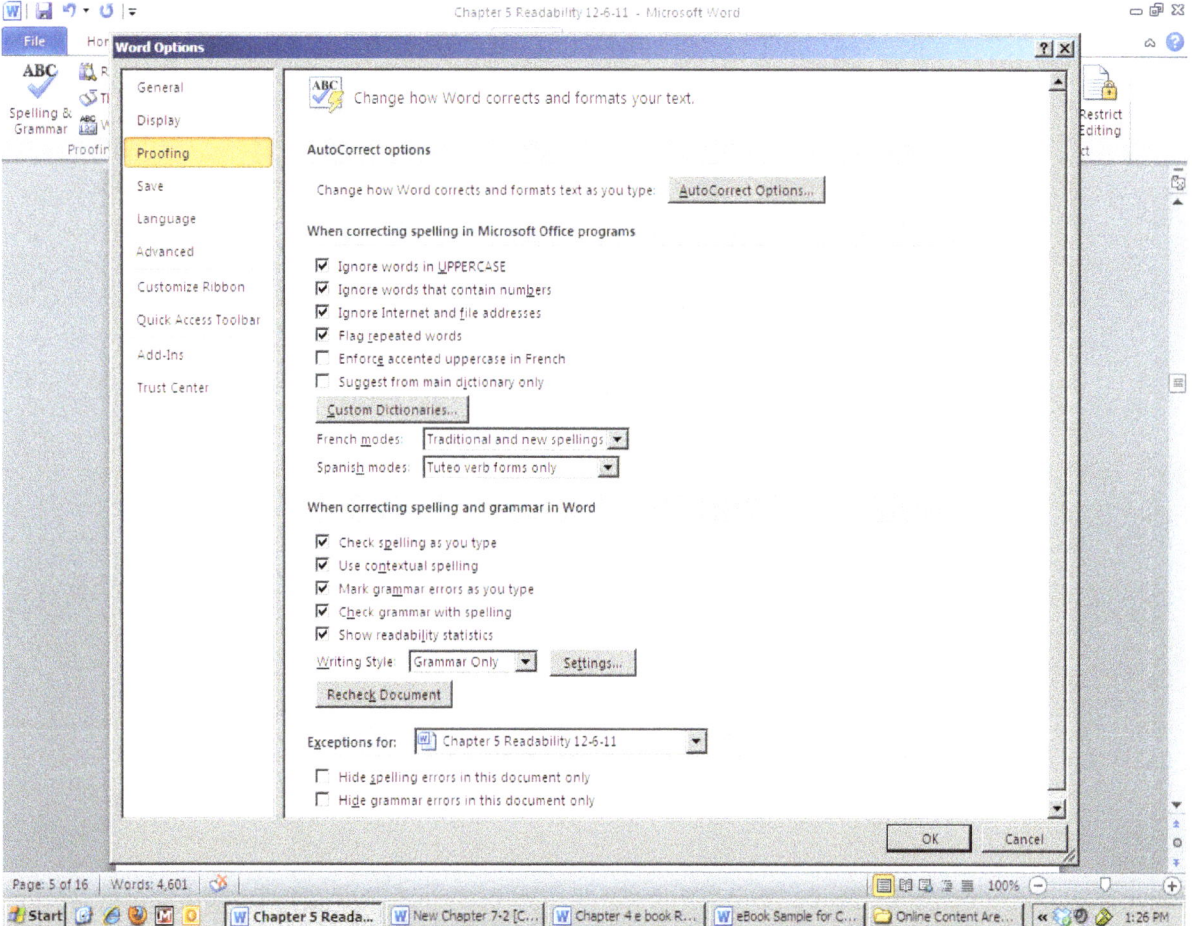

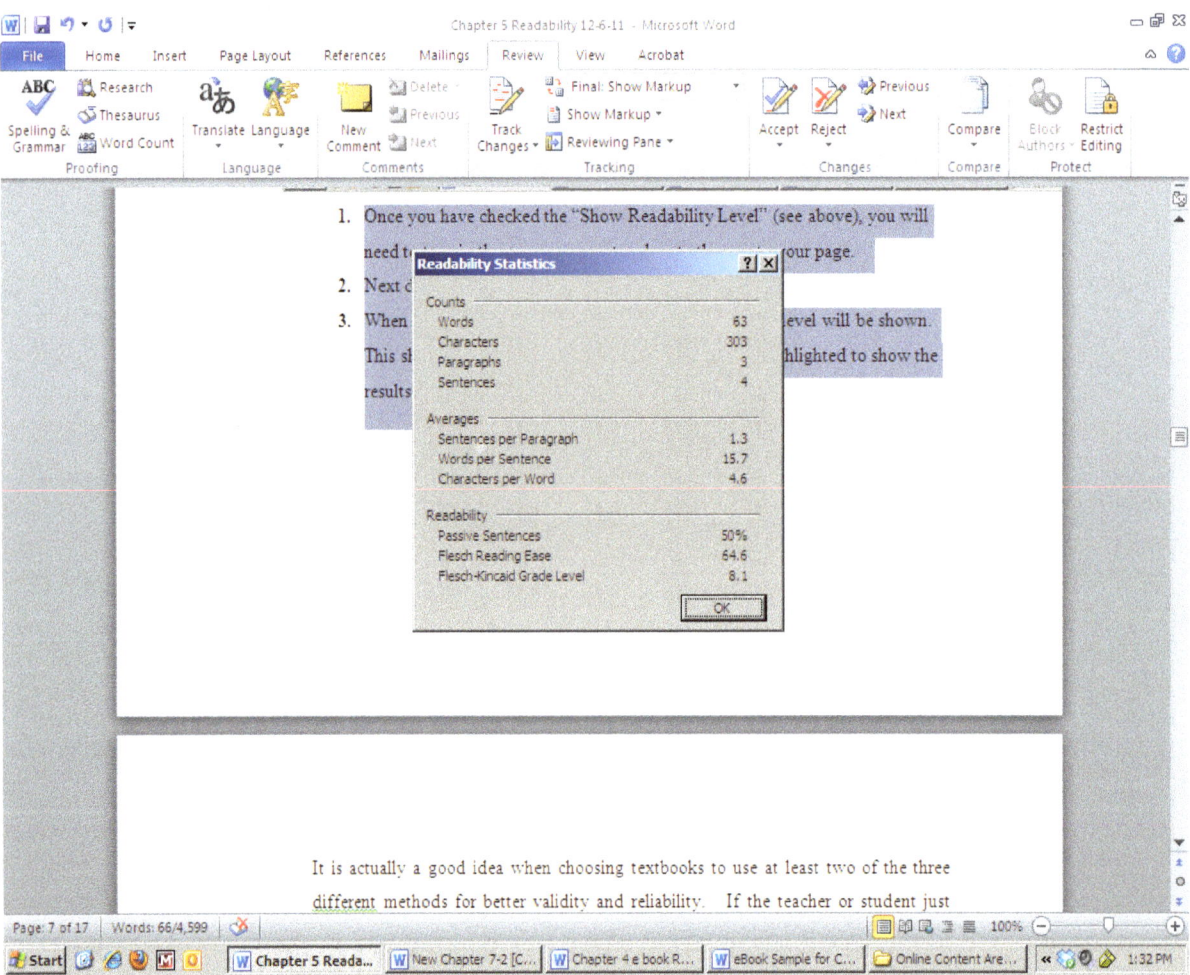

Kinkaid is usually the fastest way to determine formula readability, since the computer does all the counting for you. Although the Flesh-Kinkaid gives you additional information (such as the number of words and characters), the most useful information for you will be the reading ease percentage and grade level. Keep in mind that simply written at a lower grade-level does not mean the material is necessarily appropriate for that level. None of the formulas consider content complexity. In this latest version of Word, the Flesch-Kinkaid can be found by going on the internet to office.microsoft.com and then going to **Word 2010** (Newer versions are available). **"Readability Level"** and you will be told exactly what to do. In the **Tools** menu, under **File**, go to **Options**, then **Proofing**, and then the chart that shows a box to check readability level will appear. After you check the box, and say "ok," you still need to do a spell-check on the material you are measuring. After you highlight your material and do the spell-check, the readability formula will appear, as it does in the example above. It's always a good idea to check the readability of what you are reading. If something is written at an extremely high level that does not mean superior writing. You can do your own survey with different newspapers, textbooks and trade books to see that often, the lower reading levels exemplify better writing. If you are using another software package, go to the internet to find how to score your passage with the Flesh-Kinkaid method.

CHECKLISTS

Readability formulas are useful, but they are only part of the picture. In addition, teachers need to use checklists that ask questions about the interest, comprehension, vocabulary, format, organization, appeal/user friendliness, and other areas of a text. Some checklists involve looking at different sections of a textbook, such as the preface, the table of contents, the glossary, the bibliography, the index, and the appendix. In addition, the graphics of a textbook can be analyzed in such forms as graphs, maps, headings, pictures, summaries, exercises, fonts, bold-faced words, italicized words, pronunciation guides, and notes in margins. Copyright dates for textbooks are also important. Most educators are encouraged to use current textbooks no older than ten years. However, exceptions to this unwritten rule prevail. Some texts, such as Strunk and White's **Elements of Style (1920)**, are timeless. In addition, accuracy, a representation of different cultures, and different types of graphics for different types of learners needs to be considered.

Many checklists are available and textbooks are certainly not the only type of literacy. Trade books, films, magazines, journals, and material from the internet are just a few of the different literacy formats that should be considered. A checklist we designed uses a mnemonic term. We teach our students to remember important material through acronyms in which each letter stands for a significant feature. In this case, our acronym is WISC. It does not mean "Wisconsin", or any type of intelligence test, but rather, each letter stands for a method of reviewing the material to see if it is appropriate for the reader. After all, the readability may be at a third grade level but still be appropriate only for adults, such as much of Hemingway's writing.

WISC ACRONYM FOR READABILITY CHECKLIST

WORDS

'Words' refers to the vocabulary of the selection. Are there many technical words? Are there many words that have four or more syllables? What words are interesting, unusual, or difficult?

INTEREST

We have known for many years that the most important aspect of reading is the student's interest in the material. Why does this material appeal to a student? What features of the material can be highlighted to activate student interest? Will the material have a wide appeal to the entire class or a more narrow appeal to a particular population? Will the students be able to relate to the material? Finding material about the same subject at different reading levels is a good way to offer information about a common subject to the entire class.

SUMMARIZE

If students are able to tell you *who-what-when-where-and why* concerning what they read, then you know that they are able to comprehend most of the material. Summarizing, or being able to relate the key facts *in one's own words*, is one of the most difficult tasks of a reader. Having material that is well-organized and understandable makes the task of summarizing easier.

CONNECT

Readers need to make associations between what is being read to their personal life, to the world, and to other texts or literacy formats. These connections will help readers become more engaged in the reading and more efficient in actually learning the new information presented. Look for reading materials that support the basic principles of schema development as discussed in Chapter 4.

CHECKLIST FOR WISC ACRONYM

WORDS: VOCABULARY

1. What before reading strategies can you prepare to help your students with the vocabulary?

2. What during reading strategies can you use to help your students understand the vocabulary while they are reading your assignment?

3. What after-reading strategies can you use to make sure all students understand the material?

4. How will you differentiate to make sure all students understand the material? Are you able to substitute another piece of writing to help those readers who are at the frustration level of understanding the material?

INTEREST

1. How do you know the material interests you students?

2. What kind of an inventory can you give

the students before they read the material to determine whether or not they will be interested in the subject?

3. While they are reading the material, what types of strategies can you give the students to maintain their interest?

4. After they have finished reading the material, how can you keep them interested in understanding, retaining, and use what they have learned?

5. How can you differentiate your teaching to help all students become interested in your subject?

SUMMARY

1. In addition to having students answer the 5-W questions (who, what, where, when, and why), can they also tell you how they were able to understand the material?

2. Are the students able to differentiate the key elements from minor elements in the work?

3. Are the students able to do a Think/Pair/Share activity where they discuss the highlights of the material?

4. Are the students able to write a succinct, clear, accurate response about what they read?

5. How can you differentiate your teaching to make sure all students understand that a summary is not just parroting what they read, but being able to talk about the main points in their reading as well as offering some fresh new insight concerning what they just read?

CONNECT

1. If what you are reading is fiction, can you connect any of the characters to people you know? In what ways?

2. If the work is non-fiction, do you know anything about the people described in the article?

3. If the work is non-fiction, are you familiar with the issue and can you relate to it?

4. For whatever type of reading you are doing, are you able to connect it to other events happening in the country or the world either today or in the past?

5. Can you relate what you are reading to another literary form such as a movie, a piece of art, or some other type of electronic media?

An additional checklist, developed by Irwin and Davis (1980), which is included in the Content Area Reading, 10th Ed. text can be found at the following website: http://www.hope.edu/academic/education/wessman/2block/assignments/textbookchecklist.htm

SUMMARY

In this chapter, a variety of readability formulas and checklists were described. The readability formulas included Lexile, Frye, and Flesch-Kincaid. An original checklist with the acronym WISC was presented as a method for reviewing the material beyond readability formulas. A website was also given to link the reader to an additional checklist developed by Irwin and Davis, 1980.

USEFUL WEBSITES

http://grammar.about.com/od/rs/g/Readability-Formula.html

http://www.ideosity.com/ourblog/post/ideosphere-blog/2010/01/14/readability-tests-and-formulas

https://support.office.com/en-us/article/Test-your-documents-readability-0adc0e9a-b3fb-4bde-85f4-c9e88926c6aa

http://www.schrockguide.net/frys-readability-info.html

http://johngarger.com/articles/writing/determine-readability-using-the-flesch-reading-ease

REFERENCES

Bean, T.W. & Readence, J. (2011) *Content area literacy: An integrated approach.* Dubuque, IA: Kendall Hunt.

Farr, J. N., J. J. Jenkins, and D. G. Paterson. (1951). Simplification of the Flesch Reading Ease Formula." *Journal of applied psychology* 35, no. 5:333-357.

Flesch, R. (1949). *The art of readable writing.* New York: Harper.

Flesch, R. (1943). Marks of a readable style. (Dissertation). *Columbia University contributions to education,* no. 187. New York: Bureau of Publications, Teachers College, Columbia University.

Flesch, R. (1948). A new readability yardstick. *Journal of applied psychology* 32:221-233.

Fry, Edward. (1977). Elementary reading instruction. NY: McGraw-Hill, graph found on p.217.

Irwin, J. W. and. Davis, C. A. (November 1980). Assessing readability: The checklist approach. *Journal of Reading,* 24 (2), 124-130.

Kern, R. P. 1979. *"Usefulness of readability formulas for achieving Army readability objectives: Research and state-of-the-art applied to the Army's problems.* Fort Benjamin Harrison, ID: Technical Advisory Service, U.S. Army Research Institute. (NTIS No. AD A086 408/2).

MetaMetrics. (2011). The Lexile framework for reading.www.lexile.com

Raygor, A. L. (1977). *The Raygor readability estimate: A quick and easy way to determine difficulty.* In P. D. Pearson (Ed.) The 26th Yearbook of the National Reading conference (pp. 259-263). Clemson, South Carolina: NRC Inc.

Schrock, Kathy. (1995-2012) Kathy Schrock's guide for educators: Fry's readability graph: Directions for use. http://school.discoveryeducation.com/schrockguide/fry/fry.html

Wright, B.D. & Stenner, A.J. (June, 1998) Readability and reading ability. Paper presented to the Australian Council on Education Research. ED 435 979

CHAPTER SEVEN
DIFFERENTIATION TO MEET THE NEEDS OF ALL STUDENTS

DIFFERENTIATED INSTRUCTION

When we went to elementary school in the 50's and 60's, the current idea of differentiation wasn't a part of the general curriculum or style of instruction. Instead, we had a set curriculum and the teacher presented information in a one-style-fits-all fashion. Of course, children were grouped according to ability for reading, and each group had a specific name (The Redbirds, The Bluebirds, The Crows). We all knew exactly what each group level was, too. Then, in Paula's and Dianne's high schools, students were 'tracked' according to perceived abilities. Accelerated courses, regular courses, and remedial classes were taught in English, history, science, and math. We were in the college-bound track unlike the alternative *you're going to get a job after graduation* track.

It wasn't until 1976 that Special Education mandates were introduced with the *Individuals with Disabilities Education Act (IDEA)*. This federal law governed how states and public agencies would provide special education services to children with disabilities from birth to the age of 21. The law guaranteed students a free appropriate public education in the least restrictive environment. Free and public was easy to understand, but appropriate education was a much different matter. Some of these students needed materials presented in a different format; some of these students needed to demonstrate their mastery in a different way, and they were all supposed to do this to the greatest extent possible in the general education setting. In the last few years, however, the term *differentiation* has emerged.

Differentiation is about meeting the needs of all students. Students with disabilities and students who are gifted, students who are culturally diverse, students whose native language is not English, whether or not students are raised in comfortable homes or in Section 8 housing. Differentiation recognizes that all of these students may perform better if an individual's experiential background and current academic skills are considered when instruction is being designed. This type of instruction will present information and allow for the demonstration of mastery in a variety of ways.

Thinking/Discussion Point: Brainstorm all the words you can think of when you hear or see the term, **differentiation**. Categorize those words and label. Ask other teachers to do the same. Then look for similarities and differences between what each person has created. Discuss these similarities and differences. Is there a consensus on what differentiation means?

According to Mann, S. and Willis, L. (2000):

Differentiated instruction is a teaching philosophy based on the premise that teachers should adapt instruction to student differences. Rather than marching students through the curriculum lockstep, teachers should modify their instruction to meet students' varying readiness levels, learning preferences, and interests. Therefore, the teacher proactively plans a variety of ways to 'get at' and express learning.

And from Tomlinson (2000):

What we call differentiation is not a recipe for teaching. It is not an instructional strategy. It is not what a teacher does when he or she has time. It is a way of thinking about teaching and learning. It is a philosophy.

TO OUR MINDS, DIFFERENTIATION IS JUST GOOD TEACHING.

As you know from previous experiences and education classes, our classrooms are very diverse. Students come from different backgrounds, have different cultures, and learn in many different ways. During the late 70's through the 90's, the solution for those students who weren't achieving success in learning in the traditional way was to provide a label: learning disabled, language impaired, emotionally disordered, mentally challenged. These students were placed in resource programs or self-contained classrooms where they received special services to help them learn. Sometimes this method worked and these students were successful, but sometimes it didn't work, and the students graduated without the necessary skills for successful adulthood.

As educators became more aware of 'best practices' in pedagogy, they realized that perhaps this labeling in terms of disability was a disservice. Our students were often misdiagnosed as 'learning disabled' or 'language impaired' and removing them from the regular education classroom was not as beneficial as was hoped. We currently accept the philosophy of differentiation and have since been working out ways to make this concept an automatic part of our instructional planning.

To differentiate instruction, teachers can modify four key teaching areas:

1. **Content** (the options for <u>what</u> materials are presented)
2. **Process** (the options for <u>how</u> students learn)
3. **Product** (the options for how students tell you what they learned, and
4. **Environment** (how the classroom itself supports different styles of learning so that students are helped to learn to the best of their ability)

Tomlinson (1997) adds that five general principles need to be applied in order to make these modifications. These principles are:

1. **Have clear learning goals** based on what is appropriate for an individual student.
2. **Create respectful tasks.**
3. **Provide instruction** with an appropriate degree of challenge.
4. **Allow for flexible groupings.**
5. **Use ongoing assessments** and make **appropriate adjustments** based on assessment results.

Let's apply these principles to the general principles of content area reading instruction. The goal of your teaching is for your students to learn, to the best of their own and your ability, the content material being presented. As the teacher <u>you</u> are responsible for this learning.

Research demonstrates that students learn content information best when teachers use the instruc-

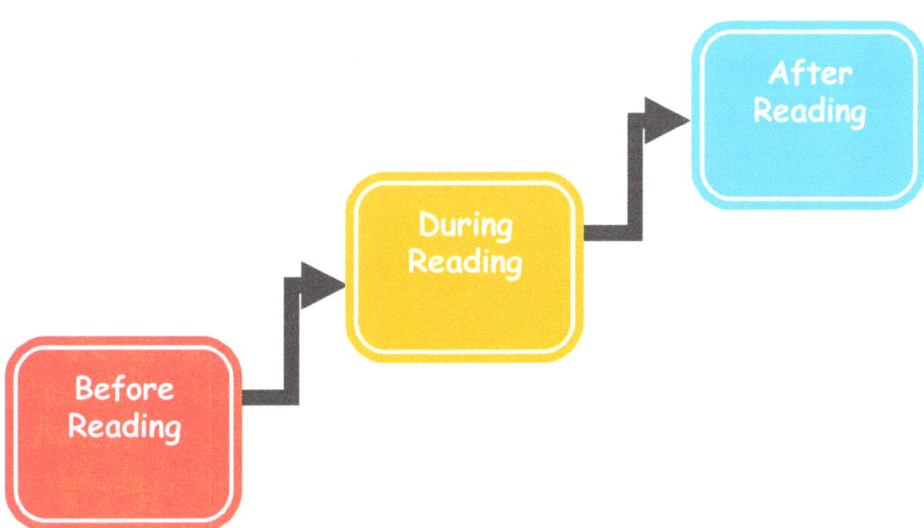

Instructional framework of Reading Process

tional framework of *Before Reading Strategies—During Reading Strategies—After Reading Strategies*. In essence, teachers are 'scaffolding' the lesson so that students can be successful learners.

Now, added to this instructional framework are the principles of differentiated instruction. All students should not be expected to learn all things at the same level of achievement. This idea doesn't mean that you need to "water down" the curriculum for some students. Instead, plan to provide different, yet appropriate challenges for <u>all</u> students.

To accomplish this result, you need to know your students and understand their different learning styles, their interests, and their particular learning needs. Your students are working at a variety of levels within your classroom. Past testing information, learning style inventories and observations can be useful tools to help you determine what these different levels are.

Next, you need to evaluate your curriculum to determine which areas could be adapted. Identify the key principles and skills that <u>all</u> students need to learn. Then decide how these major concepts could be taught by applying different levels of difficulty or complexity to each. List different activities and assessment procedures that would be of use in addressing the goals and objectives you need to teach.

Finally, think of ways in which you can vary your instruction. How will you target the different learning styles of your students? Think in terms of auditory, visual, and kinesthetic learning. How can you arrange your classroom? Think in terms of flexible groupings. How will you provide a variety of different materials? Remember to consider different reading levels. How can you organize your time in class to allow students to work on different projects in different ways? What alternative methods of assessment can you use that will allow students to demonstrate their mastery of the content at their particular level?

Thinking/Discussion Point: With the above information in mind, think about a Unit Plan that you might be creating. Examine your objectives for your Unit. Think in terms of the different learners you are likely to encounter. Regroup your objectives, and perhaps add more, to reflect the following:

A. What can **all** students learn?
B. What can **most** students learn?
C. What can a **few** students learn?

Your most gifted students should be able learn all these objectives—a, b, & c. Your average students might just be able to learn objectives a & b. Your struggling learners might only be able to learn objectives in category A.

STRUGGLING READERS

The goal of content instruction is for learners to comprehend, or understand, content information. These understandings eventually lead to being able to think about and consequently learn the content of math or science or language arts or foreign languages.

Unfortunately, students frequently struggle with the reading demands of their content classes. They often don't read the texts required in class because they <u>can't</u> read the texts. They have difficulty understanding. Break-downs in comprehension occur in three major areas (Westby, 2005):

1. Understanding of the literate language used in texts and teaching

2. Having background information, also known as 'Schema' related to the topic being addressed and

3. Having metacognition or knowledge about how one learns and what strategies need to be applied to aid in this learning when it becomes difficult. Consider the following excerpt **(Figure 1)** from a textbook on speech and language disorders.

Do you want to read on? Probably not. Perhaps you experienced some of the same frustration that adolescent readers experience when they attempt to read texts in your content area. Let's examine what happened in terms of those three areas mentioned above.

FAILURE TO UNDERSTAND LITERATE LANGUAGE

The term 'literate language' refers to the vocabulary and complex sentence structures found in many textbooks. In the passage below terms such as '*neuropathologies of speech*', '*neuropathologic syndrome*', and '*spastic dysarthria*' are not known to most. And what about '*antagonistic or spastic co-contraction of the intrinsic laryngeal muscles*'? Other words such as '*distinguish*', '*assumption*', *and* '*coincident*' are not commonly used in everyday speech. Next, look at the sentence structures themselves. The sentence beginning "One common difficulty…" takes four lines before it is completed. This, of course, is extreme. However, for those students who struggle with reading or those who just don't read and therefore are not exposed to literate language often, difficult vocabulary and long, complex sentences make it hard

> It has been common to distinguish the different neuropathologies of speech via contrastive profiles of descriptive behaviors. One common difficulty, in neurology as well as speech pathology, has been the assumption that these diagnostic indicators of a particular neuropathologic syndrome are coincident with or underlie the debilitating performance deficits associated with the disease. For example, in the person with spastic dysarthria, it has been assumed that some of the diagnostically distinct speech signs can be ascribed to hypertonicity in the form of muscle spasms. The so-called "strained-strangled voice" observed in these dysarthric persons is thought to be due to antagonistic or spastic co-contraction of the intrinsic laryngeal muscles. (Abbs & Rosenbek, Handbook of Speech and Language Disorders, p. 376)

Figure 1: A Reading Excerpt

to understand and the result is just not reading, or what we now call aliteracy. (Did you have to go back and reread that last sentence to try to make sense of it? You get the idea?)

Thinking/Discussion Point: Look through one of the texts from your content area. What do you notice about the vocabulary and sentence structures? (Note: Remember, it is not just the words in bold print that are difficult. Many of the words used to describe or discuss our content topics are hard for students not familiar with a particular type of writing. They are the words **not** commonly used in everyday talking. View this writing with a 'new eye'. While you may understand the vocabulary being used, will a young adult who isn't exposed as much to reading be able to comprehend it?)

LACK OF SCHEMA

Another common contributor to comprehension problems is lack of background knowledge or schema. According to researchers, schema is extremely important for learning new information. The term 'schema' refers to experiences, conceptual understandings, attitudes, values, skills, and strategies brought by a reader to the reading task. Without schema we would have difficulty organizing and storing new information as it is introduced. Students use schema to help them recognize the different types of genre being used. Schema also allows the reader to decide what is important, to make inferences, to summarize, and to develop good questions. The passage in Figure 1 was likely to be difficult to understand if you didn't have a background in speech pathology.

In addition, a good reader understands the differences between the type of expository text found in Figure 1 and a narrative text. As seen in **Figure 2**, there are distinct differences between narrative and expository texts. Narratives tell a story and have characters, setting, a plot and theme. Children become very familiar with narratives from an early age by listening to stories and watching movies and television shows, and in fact, the stories they tell about what they did over the weekend or the night before, are narratives. Expository texts –the textbooks used in content area classes—are very different. They are organized differently and focus on presenting factual information providing details first in order to develop a larger picture on a specific topic.

Paula remembers attempting a KWL with students in a World History class. The first question was: "What do you know about the Renaissance?" She was met with silence. That told her it was going to be difficult, if not impossible, to study that period in history if she didn't begin to develop some

Narrative vs. Expository	
Focus on character, setting, plot, antagonist, protagonist, and theme	Focuses on information
	Often used to inform
Often used to entertain or enlighten	Readers need to synthesize
Familiar organization (schema)	

Figure 2

schema on the topic for her frustrated students. She began the unit, therefore, by presenting the information in a narrative form using video clips from movies (*Lion in Winter, Michelangelo, A Man for All Seasons*), short reading passages, and pictures. After that introduction, it was much easier for students to think about the topic and go on to respond to the questions, "What would you like to learn?" and "What do you think will be important to learn?"

Dianne had a similar experience when she introduced a poem about covered bridges and discovered none of her students had ever seen one. She realized that she had to first find pictures of covered bridges and even told a story about a covered bridge in her hometown. This simple introduction made it much easier for her students to understand and relate to what was being taught.

Thinking/Discussion Point: Think about what you could do if you found yourself in the same situation as Paula and Dianne. List possible ideas for developing the students' schema on a topic in your content area.

POOR METACOGNITION:

Metacognition refers to your ability to think about and control your own reading and thinking. It includes self-knowledge about yourself as a learner as well as your knowledge about the skills and strategies that you could use when you find you don't understand what you are reading. Metacognition also involves the ability to self-monitor and regulate your own comprehension. You probably used some metacognitive strategies when you were reading the text in Figure 1. Did you recognize at what point you began to have difficulty understanding? Did you go back and reread and try to figure out the meanings of unfamiliar terms? Did you stop to think of any connections you could make between what you were reading and other experiences? If you did, you have good metacognitive skills. However, you will find that many of your students don't have this skill. They just decide to not read the assignment. You didn't do that, did you?! Or, sometimes they read it all the way through but don't understand it and think, 'Oh, well. Too bad'. Imagine!

- Students need to understand the purpose of the reading assignment.
- Students need to be able to identify the important main ideas and supportive details of a message.
- Students need to be able to focus attention on major content information
- Students need to be able to self-monitor their own comprehension.
- Students need to be able to self-question to determine if their reading goals are being achieved.
- Students need to be able to take corrective action as needed.

Figure 3: Essential Metacognitive Behaviors

Figure 3 lists important metacognitive behaviors that upper grade teachers often take for granted but shouldn't.

WHAT CAN BE DONE WHEN STUDENTS DON'T HAVE THE NECESSARY SKILLS?

DIFFERENTIATING OBJECTIVES

The first step in lesson planning is deciding on your objectives. As discussed above under differentiated instruction, you need to differentiate your learning objectives in accordance with your learners. You will have a wide range of ability levels within each of your classes. Ask yourself the following questions: 1) What can *everyone* in my class learn? All students from gifted to struggling, should be able to accomplish these objectives. 2) What can most of my students learn? This answer will exclude some of the students with specific learning deficits or problem behaviors. 3) What can just a few of my students learn? This response will allow for additional objectives for gifted learners. (*See* **Figure 4**)

DIFFERENTIATING MATERIALS

Differentiating objectives is the first step. The next step involves differentiating materials. The primary focus here is on providing different levels of reading about the topics presented in your classroom. Students should never be given reading materials that are at a frustration level. As you read in Chapter 6 on Readability, the three levels of reading

---

For this example in a unit on magnetism, all students will be assessed on the objectives listed in green. Most students, but not all, will be assessed on objectives listed in green and blue. A few students will be assessed on all objectives. (McMullen, V., 2012)

- Observe the interaction of permanent magnets with a variety of common materials.
- Discover that magnets display forces of attraction and repulsion.
- Acquire vocabulary associated with magnetism and electricity.
- Use scientific thinking processed to conduct investigations and build explanations: Observing, communicating, comparing, and organizing.
- Understand and construct simple open, closed, parallel, and series circuits.
- Measure the change in force between two magnets as the distance between them changes.
- Identify materials that are conductors and insulators.
- Experience the relationship between the number of turns of wire around an electromagnetic core and the strength of the magnetism.
- Make an electromagnet.
- Use knowledge of electromagnets to make a telegraph.

Figure 4: Setting Objectives (McMullen, V., Webster University, Personal Communication, Oct. 2010)

are the independent level, where a student is able to read material without any help, the instructional level, where the student may be able to read the material but needs some help, and the frustration level, where the student is unable to read the material at all. Figure 5 below summarizes these levels in terms of characteristics of the reader and the type of reading assigned.

Thinking/Discussion Point: When planning a unit of study, find a variety of texts at different reading levels that you can use throughout your lessons. Materials can be textbooks, on-line information, trade books, journal articles, magazine articles, and other forms of communication. Be creative and consider finding information that meets your students' needs as well as your own in terms of interest and content objectives.

ASSESSMENT ISSUES

Assessment is of key importance in education at this time. Teachers are required to have pre-assessment data, formative assessment data, and summative assessment data. **Pre-assessments** are given before the actual planning of lessons. They help you to know about your individual student's learning needs. **Formative assessments** occur throughout your lessons and help you to determine if students

Level	Characteristics	Types of Reading
Independent	• 90% + Comprehension • 99% Word Recognition • Few or no repetitions • Very fluent	• All schoolwork and reading expected to be done independently • Pleasure reading • Informational reading
Instructional	• 75-85% comprehension • 95% + word recognition • Fluent • A few unknown words • Some repetitions	• Guided reading • Basal instruction • Texts used for instruction
Frustration	• $\leq$ 50% comprehension • $\leq$ 90%-word recognition • Word-by-word reading • Many unknown words • Rate is slow • Lack of expression	• No instructional materials • Occasional self-selected materials if interest and background knowledge are high

Figure 5: Reading Levels

are making progress towards achieving the goals you've set and to adjust your teaching if needed. **Summative assessments** are used after the unit to determine if your students actually mastered the objectives that were set for them. In other words, did the students learn what you wanted them to learn? In planning we recommend beginning with your summative assessments.

The steps listed in **Figure 6** will help you to develop an assessment plan. Notice that you begin by developing your objectives first and then deciding on your summative assessments. After that, you develop your pre-assessment.

1. Think of ways for students to show that they have met the objectives that you initially determined were important for your unit. At this point just list as many ways as you can think of—don't worry about whether they are summative or formative.
2. Make sure that your ideas include all the objectives that you want to cover.
3. Also make sure that your ideas will allow all students the ability to actually show what they have learned. Some may need to be done orally, some in writing, some artistically--- another way to differentiate.
4. Based on your list of summative assessments, you can now develop pre-assessments. Your goal with pre-assessments is to find out what your students already know so that you can group them according to their level of understanding. For example, you might group according to grade level: a) above grade level, b) at grade level, c) below grade level. Using ideas from your assessments helps you remain focused on the important objectives of your lesson. It will also help you to measure progress from the beginning of the unit until the conclusion. You can demonstrate where students began in terms of their understanding and what they learned by the end.
5. Your formative assessments can be taken from the initial list you created of ways for students to show what they learn. What can you use during each lesson in your unit to monitor student learning? These assessments are important because they allow you to adjust your teaching along the way—far better than waiting until the very end to find that students haven't been understanding and learning what you wanted.

Taken from; Wormeli, R. (2007), Differentiation: From Planning to Practice, Grades 6-12. Portland Maine: Stenhouse Publishers.

Figure 6: Developing an Assessment Plan

SUMMARY

This chapter has looked at struggling readers and the issue of differentiation. Students struggle in reading primarily because of difficulty in three major areas: understanding literate language, development of schema, and metacognitive skills. Teachers can help all students—those who struggle as well as those who thrive—with differentiation in terms of content, process, the product, and the environment. An assessment plan that gathers information on student's abilities and learning pre-during and post is essential in knowing how to differentiate instruction.

Note: An excellent text to help you differentiate your instruction is Rick Wormeli's *Differentiation: From Planning to Practice, Grades 6-12.* (2007, Stenhouse Publishers). The author leads you through the process step-by step in a practical, teacher-to-teacher style that is not only easy to read, but highly informative.

REFERENCES

Mann, S. and Willis, L. Differentiating instruction: finding manageable ways to meet individual needs. *ACSD Curriculum Update*, Winter, 1-8.

McMullen, V. (2010). Personal communication, Oct. 2010. St. Louis, Webster University

Tomlinson, C. A. (2000b). Reconcilable Differences? Standards-Based Teaching and Differentiation. *Educational Leadership*, 58(1), 6-11.

Wormeli, R. (2007). Differentiation: From planning to practice, grades 6-12. Portsmouth, NH: Stenhouse.

CHAPTER EIGHT
USING TRADE BOOKS IN ALL CONTENT AREAS

One of the major problems in teaching content classes throughout middle and secondary classrooms is the reliance on textbooks. Content areas such as science, math, and social studies don't necessarily use young adult literature at all and many language arts classrooms rely on one text per unit for all students. Teacher training programs in the secondary areas do not help this situation. Most university programs only require one course in content area reading. A Young Adult Literature course is often required only for middle school students in language arts and secondary programs in English. Therefore, many middle and secondary teachers do not recognize the benefits of using trade books in their classrooms. What are trade books? **A trade book is any book that is not a textbook.**

Often, students struggle to comprehend their textbooks because they are usually not very engaging, and they are written at reading levels that students find difficult. Trade books can be used to enhance the material in the texts. Few students rave about a "wonderful textbook," but many adolescents will share their enthusiasm about nonfiction/fiction books, interesting articles in magazines, newspapers, or on social media. Today, Young Adult Literature does not merely refer to trade books, but also includes a wide range of literacies other than the textbook. By using these various literacies (trade books, blogs, tweets, and websites) teachers can enhance student understanding and appreciation in all content areas.

EDUCATIONAL GOALS AND EXPECTATIONS

Although every content area uses standards, each teacher also needs to review the goals from the content area being taught. Knowledge and application of these goals help educators use trade books and other literacies effectively. Some examples from four major content areas are described below under "National Standards." As you read through these examples, think about ways to apply them using literacies other than a standardized textbook.

NATIONAL STANDARDS:

ENGLISH/LANGUAGE ARTS AND READING

- Reviews a wide range of texts to communicate ideas
- Encourages students to experience different kinds of texts, uses their phonological awareness (their understanding the words can be broken into separate sounds) and uses critical thinking to identify elements in the text and create meaning.
- Encourages students to participate as critical members of a literacy community
- Encourages students to use language to accomplish their own purpose for understanding

MATH

- Helps students understand patterns, relations, and function while they represent, analyze, and generalize a variety of different word patterns (Algebra Standard)
- Helps students organize and consolidate mathematical thinking through communication as they communicate mathematical thoughts coherently and clearly to other students and the teacher. (Communication Standard)
- Helps students analyze and evaluate the mathematical problem-solving type of thinking and strategies of others using the language of mathematics to state ideas clearly and concisely (Communication Standard)
- Helps students to build mathematical knowledge through solving problems that occur in mathematics and other contexts and to apply and adapt different appropriate strategies to solve problems as they reflect on the process of mathematical problem solving (Problem-Solving Standard)
- Helps students use representations (KWL) to organize, record, and communicate mathematical ideas and use representations to model and interpret physical, social, and mathematical phenomena. (Representation Standard)

SCIENCE

- Students identify questions (form questions about what they want to know and look for answers to these questions) that can be answered through scientific investigations; students form questions that are relevant and meaningful; students become a community of learners when they collaborate in their search. (Science as Inquiry Standard)

- Students read to find answers in relationship to both personal and social perspectives (Science in Personal and Social Perspectives Standard)

SOCIAL STUDIES

- Include readings that allow for the study of culture and cultural diversity (Cultural Standard)
- Include readings that show how humans see themselves in and over time (Time, Continuity, and Change Standard)
- Include readings that study people, places, and environments (People, Places, and Environments Standard)
- Relate reading to your own experiences (Individual Development and Identity Standard)
- Have students make global connections based on what they have learned (Global Connections Standard)

Music, Art, Foreign Languages and other content standards can also be applied by using trade books about musical and visual artists or other visionaries from various countries. Students could listen to and appreciate the music of the artist, view pictures painted by the artist, or study the culture of the artist.

THE PHENOMENA OF HARRY POTTER

Middle school language arts teachers in a rural setting decided to use a Harry Potter book to "encourage students to participate as critical members of a literacy community". They wanted to engage their students in reading for pleasure, to learn to ask questions, to predict, and to summarize at the end of each chapter. At the beginning of each chapter, the title was read and discussed as students attempted to predict what was going to happen in that chapter. Students also looked carefully at the picture at the beginning of each chapter and tried to figure out what it was. Once the teacher began the read-aloud, students looked for answers to their questions about the picture, the title, and their prediction, based on what was previewed. While reading aloud, students who had trouble listening were encouraged to visualize what they were hearing. This method was helpful for students who tended to be easily distracted or who preferred learning spatially. Many of the students purchased the books and read ahead, just to find out for themselves what was going to happen next. Others bought books so they could follow along while the teacher was reading. Middle school students who were supervised over a two-year period read the *Harry Potter* books eight to ten times. Even though they knew what was going to happen, they loved to hear the story again and again. The power of storytelling can be just as effective with middle and high school students as it is with young children. Today, students share *Wonder* after seeing the movie and look forward to the latest sequel of the R.L.Stein's "most unfortunate events."

IMPORTANT THEORISTS FOR TODAY'S READERS: ROSENBLATT & VYGOTSKY

Perhaps one of the most important theorists of all time when it comes to reading is Louise Rosenblatt (1904-2005). During the 1930's, while she was in college and during her formative years, she knew Margaret Mead, John Dewey and Henry James, all of whom influenced her in different ways. Her first timely and timeless book, *Literature as Exploration* (1938), introduced the "READER RESPONSE" Theory, which she called a transaction between the reader and the text. She also emphasized how each person's reading of a text (which she referred to as a "poem" in her writing) was unique. These concepts were reiterated and expanded in her second major book, *The Reader, The Text, The Poem: The Transactional Theory of the Literary Work* (1978). Today, any book on reading will discuss the importance of a reader's individual background knowledge, beliefs, and context while reading a particular work, but before Rosenblatt, literary theory mainly emphasized what critics told readers a text was about. Another important contribution to the field of reading that Rosenblatt brought into view was the differences required for different kinds of reading. Rosenblatt believed there were two major types of reading. The first was for "aesthetic" purposes, or in other words, reading for pleasure. The second was for "efferent" reading, which was to obtain information or meaning. Sometimes, of course, readers can find pleasure in reading for information and the two overlap. In an interview with Louise Rosenblatt, who was a distinguished visiting scholar at the University of Miami in 1999, she said, "Each of us brings to the text the sum total of our past experiences. In that, I'm summarizing Vygotsky. Now, Vygotsky understood and emphasized very much the social character of language. But at the same time he recognized that each of us has only this personal experience which is the language for us at that moment. (March 14, 1999, retrieved 25 Sept. 2011: http://www.education.miami.edu/ep/rosenblatt/).

USEFUL WEBSITES FOR LOCATING GOOD YOUNG ADULT LITERATURE

Many different strategies can help students find outstanding fiction and nonfiction literature, such as discussing the reading interests of the students in your classroom, describing books that you (as the teacher) like now, and ones you liked as a teen. You can also get recommendations from other teachers, the community, and best seller lists. However, one of the most effective ways of reviewing good literature for young adults is to review the various websites that list a variety of categories giving award winning and honor titles to books of distinction. Some of these websites featuring award-winning books are described in Figures 1-10. Guidelines for how to select excellent books in each category are described on all of these websites.

AAAS/Subaru/Science Books and Films Prize for Excellence in Science Books*

For outstanding science writing and illustration for children and young adults (American Association for the Advancement of Science/Science Books and Films). The prizes began in 2005 by looking back on decades of outstanding science books and honoring five authors and one illustrator for their significant and lasting contribution to children's and young adult science literature and illustration. Beginning in 2006, the AAAS/Subaru *SB&F* Prize began honoring recently published, individual science books. Go to: http://sbfonline.com/prizes.htm

Alex Awards*

Annual list, since 1998, of 10 adult books that have special appeal to young adult (American Library Association/Young Adult Library Services Association). Go to: http://www.ala.org/ala/mgrps/divs/yalsa/booklistsawards/alexawards/alexawards.cfm

Carter G. Woodson Book Awards*

For most distinguished social science books beginning in 1974, that depicted ethnicity in the United States (National Council for the Social Studies). Carter G. Woodson was a distinguished African American historian and educator who wrote books for adults and young people. Go to: http://www.socialstudies.org/awards/woodson

Notable Books for a Global Society *

Annual list of "outstanding trade books, from kindergarten through high school, that enhance student understanding of people and cultures throughout the world." (International Reading Association). Go to: http://www.csulb.edu/org/childrens-lit/proj/nbgs/intro-nbgs.html

Notable (Social Studies) Trade Books for Young People *

Annual list of recommended books about social studies. (Current list available to members only.) (National Council for the Social Studies with the Children's Book Council).

Outstanding Science Trade Books*

Annual list of recommended children's science trade books each year (National Science Teachers Association with the Children's Book Council). From 1973-2002, the list was for children from grades K-8. High School students were added in 2002.

Robert F. Sibert Informational Book Medal*

For most distinguished informational (non-fiction) book by author(s) and illustrator(s) for children (American Library Association/Association for Library Services to Children). The Sibert nonfiction books have reached a high level of acclaim and many of the books can be used for middle and high school students, such as the 2001 Honor book ***Vincent van Gogh*** by Jan Greenberg and Sandra Jordan (Delacorte Press), which Dianne read aloud in one of her YA Literature courses. Although established in 1901, websites only list awards from 2001.

*All book award descriptions may be found on: http://www.education.wisc.edu/ccbc/links/links.asp?idLinksCategory=2

*Figure 1: SCIENCE, SOCIAL STUDIES, AND OTHER INFORMATIONAL BOOK AWARDS**

> **Schneider Family Book Award***
>
> For books that embody "an artistic expression of the disability experience for child and adolescent audiences." (American Library Association). Categories include: birth through grade school (age 0–8), middle school (age 9–13) and teens (age 14–18). http://www.ala.org/awardsgrants/schneider-family-book-award
>
> **Association for Library Service to Children**
>
> A compilation of recommended book lists for children and teens that contain significant content concerning cultural diversity in the areas of gender, race, and ethnicity. https://www.ala.org/ala/alsc/alscresources/booklists/booklists.htm

*Figure 2: BOOKS ABOUT DIVERSITY**

GRAPHIC NOVELS

For the last few years Dianne has been using graphic novels in her young adult literature classes. As a child, Dianne, her brother, and sister spent Sunday afternoons with a can of soda, popcorn, and huge stacks of comic books. Dianne's favorites were *Wonder Woman* and *Veronica and Archie,* whereas her brother's favorites were *Batman* and *Spiderman*. Their younger sister liked *Popeye*. Today young adults can read graphic novels that have a comic book format but are in the form of novels.

RELUCTANT READERS

In the 1980's, Dianne wrote six books for struggling readers. She test-marketed them on sixth and ninth grade students, many of whom were reading well-below grade level. These books were well-received by all the students and are still being published. In fact,

> **Great Graphic Novels for Teens***
>
> Annual list of recommended graphic novels for teens (American Library Association/Young Adult Library Services Association), established in 2007. http://www.ala.org/yalsa/great-graphic-novels
>
> *All book award descriptions may be found on: http://www.education.wisc.edu/ccbc/links/links.asp?idLinksCategory=2

*Figure 3: GREAT GRAPHIC NOVELS FOR TEENS**

> **Annual list of best books for reluctant young adult readers** (American Library Association/Young Adult Library Services Association: YALSA). The Quick Picks list, starting in 1996, awards books intended for ages 12-18, with the purpose of selecting books readers will pick up on their own and read for pleasure; the purpose of the award is to appeal to teenagers who, for whatever reason, do not like to read. Quick Picks also offers a Top Ten list, which began in 1997. "Goths, gangs, rappers and vamps reigned supreme on this year's list," said H. Jack Martin, committee chair for the 2008 awards. Since 2011 awards are divided into 3 categories: Fiction, Nonfiction and Urban Underground. http://www.ala.org/yalsa/booklists/quickpicks

Figure 4: QUICK PICKS FOR RELUCTANT YOUNG ADULT READERS

Paula used them years later with struggling readers in secondary school. The books are about teenagers but are written at the 2.5 grade level. When Dianne wrote the books, she had to calculate the grade level by using the *Fry Method* (see Chapter 6), but now the *Flesch-Kinkaid* computerized version is much faster. Perhaps the most important idea in using these books is that they look the same as books that students with average reading abilities would read. Her publisher and editors decided to use actual photos for the covers instead of art because they said struggling readers preferred to see a realistic depiction of what the books would be about. (Swenson, D. (1984). Perfection Learning)

CHILDREN'S BOOKS

Dianne started teaching high school English just after she turned 21. Some of the students in her classes were older than she was. She never considered using children's books with her middle or high school students when she first started teaching, but today she goes to schools and presents children's books to students of all ages. She also encourages the students in her young adult literature classes to consider using children's books and describes how sorry she is that she didn't initially use these books, because they can be a good source for learning and can also help students develop an appreciation for art in the excellent picture books available to them. The cliché, "A picture is worth a 1000 words," is often true with children's books.

Perhaps the most well-known award winning prizes are the Newbery and Caldecott awards. The Newbery has been described already, but the Caldecott is not often as well-known to high school teachers in all subjects. In addition, many of the books listed below also have categories for young adults.

Caldecott Medal

For most distinguished illustration in a picture book for children (American Library Association/Association for Library Services to Children). The award was named after the 19th century English Illustrator Randolph Caldecott and began in 1938. Go to: http://www.ala.org/alsc/awardsgrants/bookmedia/caldecottmedal/caldecottmedal

E. B. White Read-Aloud Awards

Annual award (established in 2004) for a picture books reflects the universal read-aloud standards that were created by the work of the author E.B. White. In 2006, in recognition of the fact that reading aloud is a pleasure at any age, the award was expanded into two categories: **Picture Books,** and Older Readers. Go to: http://theabfc.wordpress.com/the-eb-white-read-aloud-awards/org

Odyssey Award

Annual award, established in 2008, going to the producer of the best audio book for children and/or young adults (American Library Association/Association for Library Service to Children, Young Adult Library Services Association). The use of audio books is another area where children and teens who have excellent auditory skills but weak silent reading skills can benefit. Go to: http://www.ala.org/alsc/awardsgrants/bookmedia/odysseyaward

Outstanding International Books

Annual list of outstanding books first published in countries other than the U.S. and then in the U.S. in the preceding year (U.S. Board on Books for Young People). Go to: http://www.usbby.org/list_oibl.html

Teachers' Choice

Annual list of best books of the year selected by teachers (International Literacy Association with the Children's Book Council). Categories divided into Primary Readers (Grades K-2; ages 5-8) and Advanced Readers (Grades 6-8; ages 11-14). Go to: https://www.themailbox.com/learning/teachers-choice-awards

*Figure 5: CHILDREN'S BOOK AWARDS**

Theodor Seuss Geisel Award

Established in 2004 and presented in 2006 for the most distinguished beginning reader (American Library Association/Association for Library Services to Children). The Geisel Award honors the author(s) and illustrator(s) of the most distinguished American book for beginning readers in the United States the preceding year. http://www.ala.org/alsc/awardsgrants/bookmedia/geiselaward

*All book award descriptions may be found on: http://www.education.wisc.edu/ccbc/links/links.asp?idLinksCategory=2

Figure 6: CHILDREN'S CHOICE AWARDS

Children's Choice Award: Children evaluate these books and write reviews of their favorites. Since 1974, Children's Choices have been used by teachers, librarians, parents, and children. The project is co-sponsored by ILA and the Children's Book Council. The complete, annotated Children's choices reading list appears each year in the October issue of *The Reading Teacher*. Go to: www.cbcbooks.org/ccba/

Figure 7: CHILDREN'S CHOICE AWARDS

Each state also has yearly awards. In Missouri, we have the *Mark Twain Awards*. When Dianne taught in Illinois, she used the *Rebecca Caudill Young Readers' Book Award* and the *Abraham Lincoln Illinois High School Book Award*. Websites that describe current preferences as well as Classics can keep teachers and young adults updated about good books with literary merit.

Figure 8: STATE AWARDS

Coretta Scott King Awards:

The Coretta Scott King Book Awards each year recognize excellent books for young adults and children by African American authors and illustrators that replicate the African American experience. http://www.ala.org/awardsgrants/coretta-scott-king-book-awards

Asian Awards:

The Asian/Pacific American Librarians Association (APALA) began in 1980 by librarians of Asian/Pacific ancestries committed to creating an organization to meet the needs of Asian/Pacific American librarians and those who serve Asian/Pacific American communities. Awards are given to different categories, including young adult outstanding books. http://www.apalaweb.org/2015-2016-asianpacific-american-award-for-literature-winners-selected/

Hispanic Awards:

This award is named after Pura Belpré, who was the first Latina librarian at the New York Public Library. The Pura Belpré Award, began in 1996, and is presented annually to a Latino/Latina writer and illustrator whose work shows, affirms, and celebrates the Latino cultural experience in an excellent book for children and youth. It is also a division of ALA.
http://www.ala.org/alsc/awardsgrants/bookmedia/belpremedal

Native American Awards:

The American Indian Youth Literature Awards are presented every other year. These awards began as a way to identify and honor the very best writing and illustrations by and about American Indians. Books selected to receive the award will present American Indians in the fullness of their humanity in the present and past contexts.

http://www.ala.org/news/press-releases/2016/02/2016-american-indian-youth-literature-award-winners-announced

Figure 9: AWARDS OF DIFFERENT CULTURES

While teaching Young Adult literature to students for the past twelve years, Dianne made sure she included a variety of current young adult literature from other cultures as well as a timeless classic. For the classical book she used J.D. Salinger's *Catcher in the Rye* because her own son told her it was one of the best books he had ever read. Often she found different cultures and sexes responded differently to the book. Some thought Holden Caulfield, the lead character, was a spoiled brat, while others saw the suffering Holden experienced and remembered when they read as teenagers and identified with the character's problems.

An African-American book Dianne assigned was *Sojourner Truth: Ain't I a Woman?* by Pat and Fred McKissack. She knew the McKissacks who explained the lengthy research they did for the book, including traveling to the sites where Sojourner lived. Fred, a former engineer, now deceased, was proficient with the details, while Pat, the storyteller, brought the book to life. Although this book was easy reading for high school students, Dianne wanted them to be familiar with the McKissacks, who won numerous book awards and were from our area. She told students they could find many versions of the story written at higher grade levels, but the McKissack book contained authentic pictures of real people who played a part in Sojourner's life or who were active in civil rights during her lifetime.

For a Native American Book, students helped Dianne make a decision when several different book choices were available. *The Absolutely True Diary of a Part-Time Indian* by Sherman Alexie was a clear-cut winner because of the humor and empathy students shared with the main character.

Other teachers recommended an excellent Asian book that was also an important choice for teen reading today. *American Born Chinese* by Gene Yang was used to illustrate how stereotypes can be handled with a logical problem-solving solution. The author, also a math teacher, did an outstanding job in combining three seemingly separate stories into one unified whole.

Even before Oprah chose *Night* by Eli Weisel for her book club, Dianne decided to use the book. Students compared and contrasted an earlier version with the more current one. Although difficult to read, because Weisel graphically described the atrocities of the Holocaust, students said it was one of the best books they had read about the subject and intended to use it in their own classrooms.

Because Dianne taught the course, she used one of her *high-interest, low-reading level books* from her publisher's leveled reading series. Students liked to point out the various changes in terminology and understanding about teenage problems in the past 30 years.

In addition, *House on Mango Street* by Susan Cisneros, which has a Latino theme of passage, was read aloud at the beginning of each class because the chapters are short. Although not required to purchase the book, about half of the students bought it and followed along while the other half preferred to listen to the story. Even though the book was not completed at the end of the course, many additional students purchased or borrowed it from the library to finish reading the story.

Figure 10: TRADE BOOKS USED IN DIANNE'S YOUNG ADULT LITERATURE CLASSES

GENRES

Genres are different kinds of categories that may vary in content, format, style, or technique. Specific genres are listed below. **Realistic fiction** tells stories that appear believable even though the author(s) created them. They could be based on real experiences but are described in different ways from the actual episodes. **Dramas** are plays, ranging from Shakespeare's *Macbeth* to television's *Downton Abby*. **Historical fiction** is based on actual events in time that have been made into creative stories. Some of the descriptions may not even be true, even though the event occurred. **Poetry** contains intense, passionate thoughts that have been put into words that may or may not rhyme. **Fantasy** contains suspended disbelief concerning magical or supernatural incidents. The difference between fantasy and science fiction is that **science fiction** is based on actual scientific or technological theories that have been fictionalized. **Non-fiction stories** are true, such as memoires, biographies, histories, and self-help books. **Multi-cultural literature** is about different people (African, Indian, Asian, Latino) or anything that relates to a variety of different cultural or ethnic groups and their experiences, not only in the United States but in other countries as well. **Global literature** refers to the coming together of different people, different places, and various types of government. **Graphic novels** could be called long comic books. This genre can be used in both fiction and non-fiction media.

> *Genres*
>
> Realistic Fiction   Drama
> Historical Fiction   Poetry
> Fantasy and Science Fiction
> Nonfiction   Multicultural (Diversity)
> **Global**   Graphic Novels

USEFUL READING STRATEGIES WHEN USING TRADE BOOK

All of the reading strategies presented in previous chapters can be used within every content area to not only help students comprehend material but to become active readers who are able to make meaning from a variety of literacies. In addition, teachers can work together in content areas based on creating similar themes across disciplines for students to be able to see the relationships of looking at a common piece of material based on understanding (English), history (Social Studies), an artist (Art), a musician (Music), changes in environments (Social Studies) and various ways of solving environmental problems (Math).

Reading material for different purposes is the mark of an advanced reader. Yet often students see subjects as isolated components. Teachers who work together to create common strategies, themes, and literacies help students understand that they are a part of an integrated curriculum and as a result, their learning improves. Understanding and appli-

Power Point Presentations: Used to present various genres and to explain/highlight/chart literary elements such as setting, characters, plot, theme, etc.

Book Talks: Students pick a favorite fiction or nonfiction young adult book that relates to material being studied. They include background information on the author and book and then tell enough of the story to obtain class interest.

Literature Circles: The purpose of literature or inquiry circles, according to Harvey, S. & Daniels, H., (2009), is to create a special activity where teachers reallocate large amounts of class time to genuine student-led, small-group book discussions. The teacher serves as a facilitator. Literature or inquiry circles can be used in all subject areas with a variety of trade books specific to the content area. Allow four to five students to choose one of several trade books for the class and organize a book club format for sharing. Each student in the literature circle has a specific task in addition to an introduction, where the group describes the author and the book. The different roles used could include:

Discussion Director: Responsible for asking questions

Connector: Responsible for making connections that include personal connections, text to text connections, and global connections

Illustrator: Responsible for drawing or bringing pictures of different parts of the story, or showing visuals if in a smart classroom setting

Vocabulary Finder (or Enricher): Responsible for finding different words in the book that are unknown, unusual, interesting, funny, or different

Literary Luminator: Selects different paragraphs from the text to share with the class and explain why they are meaningful

Figure 11: USEFUL READING STRATEGIES

cation of the different young adult literacies presented through the use of specific common strategies offers students connections to the various subjects because they recognize they can use the same techniques to interpret meaning in different courses. When teachers work to relate their material to other subjects, whether it is in a specific piece of work or a specific strategy, not only are they integrating their curriculum, but they are offering their students a way to view their courses as a whole, rather than separate components in isolation.

CRITERIA FOR CHOOSING YOUNG ADULT BOOKS

Students in young adult literature classes can use the criteria listed in all of the preceding websites to find quality books for teens. The most important characteristics for any notable books are that young adults connect to the theme, the character, the plot, the setting, the point of view, and the style/tone of a chosen book. Books that connect students to their own experiences, even if set in different eras, that connect them to other things they have read or viewed, or that connect them to different world events have an excellent chance of being regarded as noteworthy.

Young Adults need access to a variety of genres, diversity, and reading difficulty. Inviting settings with strong beginnings and endings are important. A classic is merely a book that is beloved by people for a long period, not a dusty old ancient book. In fact, books from the 60's through the 90's, are now considered classics in young adult literature. These classics include books such as *The Outsiders* (Hinton, S.E., 1967) and *Holes* (Sachar, L. 1998). Successful books, whether fiction or nonfiction, need to contain accurate descriptions. Suspended disbelief is necessary for young people to enjoy fantasy. The more young adults read, the better critics they become.

SUMMARY

This chapter described how using trade books in all content area classes can not only help students read with more understanding but also enjoy what they are reading. Using trade books can also help struggling students comprehend their textbook, which can be one or two grade levels above the standardized reading level for the grade assigned. Extensive lists of websites were described that offer excellent and enjoyable trade books in a variety of different areas. Educational goals and expectations for different content areas were reviewed. Various young adult genres were listed and specific reading strategies that could be used with trade books were explained. Useful guides for helping teachers select trade books were also listed. Teachers were encouraged to work with their colleagues in other subjects to design common themes where trade books can enhance the curriculum.

USEFUL GUIDES FOR TRADE BOOK SELECTIONS

- The Alan Review
- American Library Association and ALSAC
- Book Links
- Book List

- Books for the Teenage Reader
- The Horn Book Magazine
- International Reading Association (IRA)
- National Council of Teachers of English (NCTE)
- National Council of Social Studies (NCSS)
- National Science Teachers Association (NSTA)
- National Council of Teachers of Mathematics (NCTM)
- The National Association for Music Education (NMNC)
- National Art Education Association (NAEA)
- School Library Journal

REFERENCES

American Association for the Advancement of Science (AAAS). http://www.sbfonline.com

American Booksellers Association (ABA). http://www.bookweb.org/

ALA: American Library Association (ALA). http://www.ala.org

Association of Library Services for Children (ALSC). African Book Awards: Africana Studies Association. http://www.alsc.ala.org

Canadian Library Association (CLA). www.cla.ca/awards/yac.htm

Carnegie Library. http://www.carnegielibrary.org/

Children's Literature Assembly (CLA). http://www.childrensliteratureassembly.org/

Colorado Business Committee for the Arts (CBCA). http://cbca.org/

Cooperative Children's Book Center (CCBC). School of Education University of Wisconsin-Madison. http://www.education.wisc.edu/ccbc/

Harvey, S., & Daniels, H. (2009). *Comprehension and collaboration: Inquiry circles in action.* Portsmouth, NH: Heinemann

Horn Book. http://www.hbook.com/

International Board on Books for Young People (IBBY). http://www.ibby.org/

International Reading Association (IRA). http://www.ira.org

Irvin, J.L., Buehl, D.R. & Klemp, R.M. (2006). *Reading and the high school student: Strategies to enhance literacy (2nd Ed.)* Boston: Allyn and Bacon

Karolides, N. J. Theory and practice: An interview with Louise Rosenblatt." *Language Arts* 76 (November 1999): 158-170. Mead, Margaret.

National Council of Social Studies (NCSS). http://www.ncss.org

National Science Teachers Association (NSTA). http://www.nsta.org

National Literacy Association. (NLA). http://www.nla.org

Philomena M. et al. **An interview with Louise Rosenblatt, distinguished visiting scholar, University of Miami 1999,** March 14, 1999, retrieved 25 Sept. 2011: http://www.education.miami.edu/ep/rosenblatt/

Rosenblatt, L. *Literature as Exploration* (1938). Literature as exploration. New York: Appleton-Century; (1968). New York: Noble and Noble; (1976). New York: Noble and Noble; (1983). New York: Modern Language Association; (1995). New York: Modern Language Association.

Rosenblatt. L. *The Reader, The text, The poem: The transactional theory of the literary work*, Carbondale, IL: Southern Illinois University Press (1978). Carbondale, IL: Southern I Illinois University Press (reprint 1994).

CHAPTER NINE
MEDIA LITERACIES: THE NEW LITERACIES

When Paula and Dianne were children, television was just coming into play. In fact, Dianne's father did not even get one of the first television sets; she was eight before they bought a television with a 23-inch screen, which was then considered large. Paula remembers watching television with her family when she was about three. They watched *I Love Lucy, Howdy Doody,* and *Sheila, Queen of the Jungle*. Television for both Dianne and Paula was then only in black and white and there were only three channels: ABC, NBC, and CBS. Of course, "The Ed Sullivan Show" was a big hit for both of them, especially when the Beatles performed. Other favorites were the Saturday Night Hit Parade of the ten top tunes of the week and a fifteen-minute show featuring Nat King Cole. Obviously, not a lot of choices were available compared to the vast array of cable networks and streaming sites today. Also, with new, large flat screens and excellent color in DVD, state of the art television, will only continue to improve.

Paula and Dianne always loved music, which is quite common for children and teens. While growing up, they listened to the radio for top tunes. Now, they and most young people download lyrics onto iPods, or stream music into cell phones, iPads, and computers. Fortunately, in the small Midwestern area where Dianne lived, her father made sure they had tickets to all the major events at the local high school, which included an outstanding choir and a symphony from a private college as well as Shakespearean plays by established actors. During elementary school, all of the children in Dianne's family read every book in the school library. Of course, the library was only a small room, but the race to see who could finish reading all the books first was always a great deal of fun. They all did book reports at school, which were quite traditional, but getting that gold star at the top was a real reward. In addition, Dianne, along with her brother and sister, was fortunate to have a teacher during middle school who valued reading, writing, and viewing. The teacher who taught the upper grades (sixth, seventh, and eighth) also directed musical theater for the students. When these plays were performed, not only the parents, but the entire community came to watch them. In the seventh grade, this teacher read an assigned paper Dianne had written to the entire class, without naming the author. From that day forward, Dianne knew she was a writer. Paula remembers her parents reading aloud to her and her favorite teachers were those who spent time reading out loud to the whole class. Her good friend loved to read also, and they spent hours reading together: series books such as *Anne of Green Gables*, *Cherry Ames*, and *Nancy Drew* were some of the favorites. Dianne and Paula learned early how important it was for a teacher to encourage students in their literacy strengths.

ALL STUDENTS HAVE LITERACY STRENGTHS

Today we know that most students have some type of literacy strength. Besides the obvious reading and writing skills, many other types of literacies are also acknowledged. Perhaps it is the art of being a good listener, a good speaker, or a good conversationalist. Perhaps it is being able to reflect and think about experiences. Perhaps it is viewing films critically. Or it may be one of the many different technology literacies that are a part of all of our lives today. When Dianne completed her Ph.D. in the 90's, she was able to use many databases effectively, but she still had to go through the librarian at her university to obtain primary materials. By the time Paula completed her Ph.D. in 2004, she could find all primary sources herself in the various databases and search engines.

Every day technology is changing the way we use various literacies. We may read books on a kindle, nook, or iPad, listen to music on our iPods, subscribe to iTunes and order different apps, ranging from playing solitaire to using an online datebook or ordering a book of poetry. We take notes during class on our computers, chromebooks, and iPads, use Facebook and Twitter to communicate with others, use Webquest to help with assignments, design web pages for students to use, create wikis to allow students to work together on topics they choose related to the course, listen to other podcasts and create podcasts on areas of our own expertise; create, watch, and use YouTube in our classrooms, order products online, teach courses online, do many of our technology tasks on our cell phones and iPads; use our GPS systems to find various locations, and pay our bills and do our banking online. We often spend a good part of our day with the various media literacies, such as checking our emails, working on projects, blogging, and communicating with others through technical means

EVIDENCE BASED RESEARCH SUPPORTS THE USE OF DIGITAL LITERACY

- According to Leu (2010), the nature of reading is changing and our challenge today is in recognizing the need for an increase in professional development for educators in order to improve their use of technology in the classroom. He cautions that online and offline reading comprehension is not the same and requires different skills, and that it is important to prepare young people in using online information.

- Chandler-Olcott & Mahar (2003) state that skilled teachers should take advantage of their learners' expertise in technology and use it to create more complex contexts for literacy and learning. Luke (2007) points out students can become more successful as educational systems align with 21st century technologies, and Rich (2008) states that the Web inspires teenagers to read and write, benefiting from quickly finding different points of view on a subject and conversing with others online.

- Jones-Kavelier and Flannigan (2008) believe that literacy for young people today is dependent on understanding of high-tech realities and the development of the skills to use these effectively.

- Tierney (2009) says, after reviewing various literacy scholars, he found that students who had access to multimedia tools were able to explore, express and expand their sense of identity. Furthermore, Tierney noted that various media forms have now become part of our standard curriculum because their learning benefits have been discovered.

O'Brien and Scharber (2008), while editors of the *Journal of Adolescent and Adult Literacy*, defined digital literacies in combination with using multimodal texts. In multimodal composing and reading, they discuss how ideas and concepts are represented with print texts, visual texts (photographs, videos, animations), audio texts (music, audio narration, sound effects), and dramatic or other artistic performances (drama, dance, spoken word). From a digital framework these editors view text as providing a multimodal intentional representation with purposes and boundaries understood within a given socio-cultural domain. They also define *digital literacies* as socially situated practices supported by skills and strategies that represent an understanding of ideas using a range of modalities that incorporate a wide range of digital tools. They refer to *digitally literate people* as not only being able to select all the different types of media available but also knowing how to plan and use a variety of different media forms to show students how different types of media literacy can most clearly and accurately represent ideas. Their ideal model would combine the various traditional print literacies with a variety of media forms that engage students and help them understand how important it is in today's world to apply the many varieties of digital literacies currently available to them.

Leu, D.J., et. al, developed an excellent framework for critically evaluating websites. Their advice was put into the form of a framework published in *Comprehension instruction: Research-based best practices* (2008), Guilford Press. When looking at websites the reader needs to consider four major areas:

1. Bias and Stance of the Author
2. Reliability of the information
3. Accuracy in terms of what is being stated
4. Synthesized information or how multiple sources are brought together

Another useful way to help students determine the quality of various forms of literacy is to have them compare and contrast various medias such as television reports, online newspapers, and Facebook, to see how they cover major local news, national news, and world news.

An interesting and often humorous activity is to introduce technical vocabulary words and then go around the room, having each student take the words in order and create a sentence using the word. When all of the words have been used, the teacher can read the entire "story" to the class. Always begin the story with "Once upon a Time," and end it with, "….and they lived happily ever after….", then adding the last word on the list. Let's assume our students know several technology words highlighted below but not all that are listed. Here is a story they might compose:

Once upon a time, a community decided to do all of their small town's work by only using technology. The members of the community all got on Facebook, so they could communicate with one another. They also used email to send one another messages. Each member of the community also created a Twitter account so they could write what was happening in the community. They pinged one another on Facebook. They also sent out podcasts to show their expertise on a subject. They even created web pages to let everyone know where to go to get their groceries, gasoline, and other utilities. However, sometimes, when the online system was not working, they became frustrated. Even when they used their cell phones to call or text on another, they discovered that no one knew what was going on. Once their computer system was restored, they used search engines to help them do their work. They even went to Webquest for information. However, they discovered that what was missing was face-to-face communication, and they did not live happily ever after; in fact, their community disintegrated.

When reviewing this story, the teacher can easily see that students are familiar with most of the technical words that are highlighted. However, they did not recognize, "ping" but were able to make a good guess, just by using context. Nevertheless, the story does point out an important concept. Technology is a tool, not an end in itself. After students compose this story themselves without first going over the definitions in class, these technical vocabulary words can be introduced. Although detailed information about all of the following terms may be found on the Internet, to help our students understand the different forms of literacy, the following are several short dictionary definitions of terms we use in our classrooms:

 Apps: Short for application programs. You can purchase applications for the ITunes apps store or through Windows. Google also has apps. These apps continue to improve and offer a variety of selections, ranging from datebooks to games, eBooks and other programs.

 Android: A new, advanced type of mobile phone. Android is a free Linux-based open-source platform for mobile phones developed by Google™ and the Open Handset Alliance™, a group of 65 technology and mobile companies. Designed to optimize memory and hardware resources in a mobile environment, Android allows for smoother PC-like functionality. This device can be reformatted into different screens and offers an extremely large amount of apps. Essentially, an Android is like having your own mobile computer. (Smart phone).

 Blog: Today, it is easy to begin a blog site and many of your students probably already have one. The blog is an online personal journal with reflections, comments, and often hyperlinks provided by the writer. (tumblr.com)

 Database: The educational databases in our school and others in the area are extensive. They contain a large collection of data organized especially for rapid search and retrieval. Databases are usually the most accurate form of research, because they are more highly scrutinized than search engines. Also, data bases continue to allow more full text to be downloaded to individual computers. (jstor.com)

ebooks: An electronic version of a printed book read on a computer or handheld device.

 Email: Established in 1982, e-mail became the essential communication format throughout the 90's and is still heavily used in business and education. Most items that formerly came in hard copies are now only on e-mail, which means employees, need to constantly address their daily mail.

 eReader: An electronic device that allows users to store and read a number of books and other literary media. Popular devices are the Kindle, the Nook and the iPad. The books stored on these devices are called eBooks or electronic books.

Facebook: A popular social networking site founded in 2004 by Mark Zuckerberg. It initially targeted Harvard students, but was later opened to other universities and then high schools. In 2006, Facebook allowed everyone to join and also added a News Feed feature that broadcasts changes in members' pages to all Facebook users identified in their personal network of friends. These changes turned Facebook into a personalized social news service.

Google doc: A way to share your documents with other Google docs users.

Hashtag: Used on Twitter, the number symbol (#) is a new way to add a thought, part of a thought, or a sentence, to make it clearer and sometimes funnier. Can also be found on Facebook.

HTML: Hypertext Markup Language. First defined in 1989, this is a database format in which information related to that on a display can be accessed directly from the display; *also*: material (as text) in this format. (iconspedia.com)

Hypertext: a method of storing data through a computer program that allows a user to create and link fields of information at will and to retrieve the data non-sequentially. (eu.fotolia.com)

Hulu & Netflix: Websites that provide movies and Television shows. A charge is required for quality videos.

Instagram: An app that offers a way to photograph on smartphones.

iCloud: Stores all electronic data on an offsite server for safe-keeping and can be accessed by any device synced to your account.

iPad: The iPad (originally introduced in 2010) has a similar interface to the iPod touch and iPhone, but the larger screen allows users to substitute it for some laptop applications. The iPad was made for browsing the web, for reading eBooks (books ordered and read on the iPad) and entertainment.

iPhone: The *iPhone* is a line of internet and multimedia-enabled smartphones designed and marketed by Apple Inc. The iPhone, first marketed in 2007, has become enormously popular and more advanced with each update. Their current photo system is used by professional photographers. A large variety of apps, as well as internet service and email can be downloaded and additional platforms can be added. (Smart phone).

iPod: The iPod is a pocket device used to download music

iTunes: iTunes is a popular media player software from Apple for Mac and Windows; iTunes is widely used by millions of people to organize the music they play on the computer as well as all the content they download to their iPods, iPhones and iPads. It integrates Apple's online store for purchasing songs, videos and applications, and it administers the copy protection that was formerly applied to purchase songs. Although introduced in 2001 for the Mac, a Windows version was added in 2003. As of today, because of Windows' dominance, more people use iTunes on Windows than they do on Mac computers, but both are highly popular.

Kindle (Kindle Fire): Amazon-designed, hand-held devices of a vast number of eBooks. Also can be used as a substitute for some laptop applications.

Microsoft: A software* company that is known for the PC computer and the Windows software. Available now is Windows 8 which is an attempt to compete with Apple. They also have tablets similar to the iPad. * Software refers to the applications that run on Microsoft and Apple computers.

Ping: An internet utility used to check the connection with another site. It bounces a signal off the remote site and shows you how long it took to complete the round trip each time. If you get no returns at all, the site is either down or unreachable. However, Apple's iTunes' ping site lets you follow favorite artists and see your friends' favorites as well.

Pinterest: A way to collect a variety of items and organize them into groups.

Podcast: a program (as of music or talk) made available in digital format for automatic download over the internet.

Selfie: Taking a picture of oneself or with others and posting it.

Tumblr: A free, social networking websites that lets users post their blogs and chat with one another.

Twitter: Twitter is an information network that connects us to the latest information about what we need to find information about or whom you find interesting. By going to the web and searching for Twitter conversation from businesses and schools to celebrities, friends, professionals, and even your next door neighbor, you can follow conversations and even "Tweet." which means adding your own comments. Since Twitter focuses on real-time information, the information will be current. Each Tweet is 280 characters in length. You don't have to build a web page or even tweet to anyone to look-up information on Twitter. Dianne and Paula find Twitter to be helpful to teachers, who can send twitter messages to parents and also to teachers who wish to share information with one another. Twitter can be a good way to help tighten up writing.

YouTube: A global, video-sharing website.

Web page or webpage: a document or information resource designed for the World Wide Web (Internet). Web pages are found by using browsers from various web servers, such as Google, Yahoo, and Bing. These page(s) can be viewed on a computer monitor or cell phone. Often web pages incorporate style sheets and images, which they put in Hypertext. Since web pages can be designed by anyone, it is important for students to be able to critically assess various websites. Some web servers are private networks and known as the intranet instead of the internet. They can only be accessed at the location of the source. Corporate and academic intranets are very popular. (777icons.com)

Webquest: A *webquest* is an educational device used for the purpose of teaching students to research information and find correct answers to questions online. (webquestdirect.com)

Wiki: This feature allows our students to contribute and collaborate on topics about one subject that interest them. (pbworks.com)

Thinking/Discussion Point: Discuss which of these terms you would use in your content area and explain how you would use it. Are there any additional terms you use in social media and how do you use them?

WARNING!!

Remember, many of your postings are available to everyone. An Internet site you create can still be found years later. Blogs you created several years ago which you do not think are currently appropriate stay on the Internet. Email, Facebook, texting, and the many forms of technological advances are **NOT PRIVATE**. Inappropriate pictures posted on Facebook during your teenage years can be accessed by a future company years later and prevent you from obtaining a job. Even worse, bullying online has become illegal, after the horrendous consequences of teens who committed suicide when reading horrible attacks about themselves online.

WARNING

While *Wikipedia* is a useful source to use when reviewing information, it is still not acceptable in formal academic papers because, although the content has improved greatly over the past few years, it does not proclaim that material accepted is necessarily factual. Using this source to locate information of interest is fine, but do not use it in your formal writing as an authentic source. Wikipedia is heavily used today and will be one of the first engines that pop up on your screen when you seek information. However, **that does not mean it is the best source.**

SUMMARY

This chapter explored all the various types of media literacies and how to use them. These include digital libraries, databases, search engines, social media, smart phones, and other electronic forms electronic forms of communication.

USEFUL MEDIA LITERACY WEBSITES

http://medialiteracyproject.org/learn/media-literacy

http://www.ncte.org/lessons/media-literacy

http://www.pbs.org/pov/educators/lesson-plans.php?search_type=subject&subject=media_literacy#.VXCKq9JViko

http://www.projectlooksharp.org/?action=-generalmedialiteracy

REFERENCES

Block, C. & Parris, S. (2008). Comprehension instruction: Research-based Best practices. NY: Guiford Press.

Chandler-Olcott, K., & Mahar, D. (2003). "Tech-savviness" meets multiliteracies: Exploring adolescent girls' technology-related literacy practices. *Reading Research Quarterly,* (38)1, 356-385.

Jones-Kavalier, B. R. & Flannigan, S.L. (2006). Connecting the digital dots: Literacy of the 21st century. *Education Quarterly* (29), 2.

Leu, D. J. (2010). The future of reading: Misalignments of public policy, assessment, and instruction in an online world of new literacies, *School Library Journal's Leadership Summit 2010:* The Future of Reading.

Luke, A. (2007, May 31). The New Literacies. In *Webcasts for Education.* http://resources.curriculum.org/secretariat/may31.shtml

O'Brien, D. & Scharber, C. (2008, Sept.). Digital literacies go to school: Potholes and possibilities. *Journal of Adolescent and Adult Literacy:* (52)1, 66-68.

Rich. M. (2008) Literacy Debate: Online, R U Really Reading? In *The New York Times/Books.* http://www.nytimes.com/2008/07/27/books/27reading.html

Tierney, R.J. (2009). The agency and artistry of meaning makers within and across digital spaces. In S.E. Israel & G. G. Duffy (EDS). Handbook of research on reading comprehension (pp. 261-288. NY: Routledge .

CHAPTER TEN
STEM AND STEAM: ACRONYMS TO USE IN YOUR TEACHING AND LEARNING

STEM

STEM is actually an acronym in which each letter represents the following areas: science, technology, engineering, and mathematics. Key factors for STEM schools are inquiry, logical reasoning, collaboration, and investigation. The goal of STEM education is to prepare students for post-secondary study and the 21st century workforce.

STEM STANDARDS OF PRACTICE:

STEM Standards include the following:

1. Learn and Apply Rigorous Science, Technology, Engineering, and Mathematics Content
2. Integrate Science, Technology, Engineering, and Mathematics Content
3. Interpret and Communicate STEM Information
4. Engage in Inquiry
5. Engage in Logical Reasoning
6. Collaborate as a STEM Team
7. Apply Technology Appropriately

(http://www.marylandpublicschools.org/MSDE/programs/stem/)

The purpose of establishing a STEM school is quite obvious. The United States has fallen behind other countries in all of these areas. Each of these subjects is a necessity and involves understanding how to read the language of a particular subject. Students interested in any of these areas can select schools that have partnered with universities to offer not only rich, but rigorous curriculums. High expectations are set for all students, not only in their participation, but in their performance of project-based learning. In addition, students in STEM schools are not only prepared for the challenging courses they will experience in university settings, but also to work on projects they can present in the real-world setting to companies and organizations in these areas. Last year the highest rated STEM school in the nation, according to U.S. News and World Report, was High Technology High School in Lincroft, New Jersey. Jonathan Olsen and Sarah Mulhern Gross, who team-teach an integrated humanities program to ninth grade students at High Technology. Jonathan and Sarah are regular contributors to the New York Times Learning Network. Jon, the district's curriculum coordinator, teachers world history; Sarah, a National Board Certified teacher, teaches English.

Although these teachers select the top students in the area for their program, their description of the **five reading habits** all teachers can incorporate into their classroom is extremely useful:

1. **Read early, read late, read often**
2. **Write daily**
3. **Line up your pencils, or "Be prepared"**
4. **Collaborate with others**
5. **Question your teachers**

(Posted by Valerie Strauss, Feb. 20, 2013 in http://www.washingtonpost.com/blogs/answer-sheet/wp/2013/02/20/five-habits-of-great-students-lessons-from-top-ranked-stem-school/)

Dianne and Paula spent several months researching STEM schools. We learned that in our own state, we already have STEM schools, both in suburban and inner city settings. (http://www.stem-school.com/schools/missouri)

Teachers in these schools are trained to work together to offer their students the ability to understand theory and practice in these four essential fields. What content area teachers are now encouraged to do is to apply successful STEM practices of inquiry, logical reasoning, collaboration, and investigation. We encourage our students to:

- Obtain the necessary knowledge required in their subject area

- Offer best practice through the reading of the "languages' each subject possesses and allow their students to create meaningful projects, based on reading complex material and applying it to real world situations

Since all students cannot attend a STEM school, we believe that the successful experiences documented by these schools need to be incorporated in every science, technology, engineering, and mathematics classroom. Few of our current schools even have content area "engineering," which means that this subject can be incorporated in science, in technology, and in mathematics. All of our research indicated that the earlier children are exposed to these four content areas, the more interested in them they will become. Several schools have already begun to incorporate these subjects into their elementary and middle school curriculums. What this change means for elementary and middle school teachers is an understanding of subject matter, an ability to read the language of each of these subjects, and the ability to incorporate the principles of STEM. Giving students choices in creating projects and bringing in material about these subjects can actually be incorporated in all content areas. In Dianne's graduate **Content Area Reading** class, she introduced this topic to her students. Normally, at least a few of the students were already well aware of STEM and several had even begun to use it, particularly in mathematics and technology. By offering all students the ability to create their own final unit, whatever their subject, Dianne received creative, innovative projects that indicated successful reading and application of the STEM standards. One of the assignments in this course already asks students to incorporate technology into selected trade books from their content area. We have always stressed the importance of the concept that **all content area teachers are teachers of reading.** Now, with new CORE Curriculum requirements, as well as the new STEM and STEAM initiatives, both Dianne and Paula find that their students, once they understand the usefulness of these concepts, embrace them and, more importantly, apply them in their own classrooms.

STEAM

The acronym STEAM reflects both the international movement to add an "A" letter in the middle of the title to represent the arts — which can include the fine, language and musical arts — to STEM education and the school's desire to help students pursue a different kind of 3D: discovering, designing and developing. (Delaney M., 2014, www.edtechmagazine.com).

STEAM offers teachers and learners a way of seeing how the inter-relationships of all subjects relate in real-life. STEAM-style education can be more interesting and enjoyable in offering new ways to combine subjects within our established form of education. STEAM has been used as a tool for schools to use that keeps useful current elements while transitioning and evolving to a new multi-disciplinary format that is much more engaging and worthwhile to students because they understand how all subjects relate to one another and can be used in conjunction with one another, not as isolated units of study and practice. Good teachers, of course, are already doing this, but a stronger science, technology, and engineering background produces stronger and more useful program. According to some sources (www.smithsystem.com/stem-environment/) STEAM was developed in 2006 by Georgette Yakman, (www.iteea.org), who then was a master's graduate student at Virginia Polytechnic and State University's Integrated Science-Technology-Engineering-Mathematics Educational program (ISTEMed). Her definition of STEAM was: Science & Technology interpreted through Engineering & the Arts, all based in Mathematical elements. Since then she has continued to evolve the concept by including more research and practice on the topic. She says that she has used STEAM with significant results as a full-time middle-school and high-school teacher and as an educational consultant.

SUMMARY

This chapter described two recent acronyms and how teachers can use them in their classrooms. STEM is an acronym in which each letter represents the following areas: science, technology, engineering, and mathematics, whereas STEAM reflects both the international movement by adding an "A" letter in the middle of the title to represent the arts — which can include the fine, language and musical arts — to STEM education and the school's desire to help students pursue a different kind of 3D: discovering, designing and developing.

REFERENCES

Delaney, M. (April 9, 2014). 7 guidelines for building a STEAM program, in *Ed Tech Magazine*: http://www.edtechmagazine.com/k12/article/2014/04/7-guidelines-building-steam-program

Strauss, V. (Feb. 20, 2013) citing Jonathan Olson (@jonathanolson.com) & Sarah Mulhern Gross (@thereadingzone). http://www.washingtonpost.com/news/answer-sheet/wp/2013/02/20/five-habits-of-great-students-lessons-from-top-ranked-stem-school/

Messier, N. The how's and why's of going 'Full STEAM ahead in your classroom.' www.edsurge.com http://pgsteamteam.blogspot.com/2011/09/our-definition-of-steam-education.html Retrieved on 11/26/16

STEM education. www.marylandpublicschools.org/ Retrieved on June 20, 2018.

http://www.stemschool.com/schools/missouri/ Retrieved on 5/14/16.

www/iteea.org/ Retrieved June 20, 2018.

www.smithsystem.com/stem-environment/ Retrieved on 5/14/16.

CHAPTER ELEVEN
PUTTING IT ALL TOGETHER

The purpose of this chapter is to review states' standards in developing lesson plans and units while helping teachers understand the necessity of testing without spending months "teaching to the test".

Gardner, H. (1993) refers to intelligence as **a product that is valued in a society.** By using this definition, teachers give students choices in using their strengths. English and Math concepts are not being neglected in this model. They are still of major importance. But other intelligences, such as interpersonal, intrapersonal, musical, bodily-kinesthetic, naturalistic, and spatial can also be recognized and celebrated. These intelligences also correspond with content area subjects such as Math, Music, Physical Education, Science, and Social Studies. Carl Jung (1971) did extensive work on personality preferences, followed by Joseph Cambell in *The Portable Jung* and Briggs (1980) in *Gifts Differing*. They believed that an accurate understanding and application of personality preferences are major factors in determining success.

In our society, who makes the most money? Most of us would say people such as Bill Gates, a college dropout who used the logical-mathematical and naturalist (science) intelligences to design Microsoft. Warren Buffet also uses logical-mathematical intelligences as well as the inter- and intra- personality intelligences to determine what companies to buy and sell, and Oprah Winfrey, who did not attend college, used her interpersonal and intrapersonal intelligences to build a media empire. Musicians, specialized doctors, CEOs, sports figures, actors and talk show hosts also earn enormous salaries. In other words, our society rewards people who may excel in other areas and may even be weak in English and/or Math. By using differentiation (discussed in Chapter 7) and giving students choices, we can make a difference as in Pablo Casal's (1970) goal "to make the world "worthy of its children."

Thinking/Discussion Point: Describe what really interests you. Is it sports, art, books, movies, dance, technology, science, math, languages, English or a media source such as Facebook or Twitter? Explain why it is of interest to you and how you use it.

NATIONAL STANDARDS, STATE STANDARDS, SCHOOL DISTRICT STANDARDS, AND CORE CURRICULUM STANDARDS

Both Dianne and Paula believe in having credible standards. The International Literacy Association (ILA) and National Council of Teachers of English (NCTE) have combined to offer 12 standards on the following website: (http://www.ncte.org/standards). All content area subjects have a National organization with professional standards that preservice and practicing teachers can use.

In addition to these important National Standards, state standards are also important. Our state site (http://dese.mo.gov/) offers standards that meet specific requirements or assessments, as do many other states.

LITERACY COACHES

The International Literacy Association (ILA) defines a *literacy coach* or a *reading coach* as *a reading specialist who focuses on providing professional advice to help teachers in all content areas improve the way their students understand and apply material from their individual subjects.* (2016). Currently many school districts are working to improve adolescent literacy. The programs designed support staff for professional development for teachers, administrators and other key people who play a part in the academic program of the district. Helping these individuals learn strategies, based on sound theories that will improve literacy and content learning for all students means participation in many levels. The literacy coaches are trained to provide leadership for the district's literacy program by offering teachers specific strategies that can improve an instructor's teaching.

A successful literacy coach's role is collaborative. Coaches who are seen as advisers, helpers, and even mentors who understand the problems and the goals of both administrators and teachers are the most successful. However, when literacy coaches are viewed as supervisors who evaluate performance, teachers often become resistant to any help that may be offered. The job of a good literacy coach is to learn what the administrators want and what the teachers want and then develop ways of helping both parties achieve their needs as well as offering new, innovative ideas that will improve student learning.

When Dianne was a reading specialist, she vividly remembers her most successful experience was with Carla, an elementary school teacher, in a school that focused on multiple intelligences. Although Carla taught fourth grade students, the design of their reading/language arts program could easily be applied to middle and upper grade students. This team-taught model of an independent reading program allowed students to excel and was one which they also enjoyed. Not only were the students motivated, but they learned various useful literacy strategies and improved their standardized and individualized reading scores. (See Appendix: Carla Interview)

SUMMARY

Dianne and Paula have been working on this book for several years, because not only are they deeply interested in the topic of Content Area Literacy, but they also want it to be relevant to you. They continue to work at providing the most important tools you need to become a successful instructor of reading, no matter what content area you teach. Good luck! Of course, you may find some sections more difficult, just as we did when spending countless hours of research. But when the process involves offering a project based on sound theory and best practice, we continue to stay passionate about this topic. One of our goals is to help you become lifelong readers and learners. Another goal is that we want each one of you to be the best teacher, student, and reader you can possibly be. At one of the schools where Dianne was a reading specialist, the motto was to have the students do "their personal best." We wish the same for you.

REFERENCES

Briggs, K. & Meyers, P. (1980, revised by I. Meyers with P. Meyers in 2010). *Gifts differing.* Consulting Psychological Press (CPP): Mt. View, CA

Casal, Pablo. (1970). *Joys & Sorrows: Reflections.* NY, NY: Simon & Schuster.

Gardner, H. (1993). *Multiple intelligences: The theory in practice, a reader.* NY, NY: Basic Books

Gardner, H. (2011). *Frames of mind: The theory of multiple intelligences.* NY, NY: Basic Books

Gardner, H. (2008). *Multiple intelligences: New Horizons in Theory and Practice.* NY, NY: Basic Books

http://dese.mo.gov/ Retrieved on 1/10/17

https://www.ILA. Retrieved on 1/10/16. International Literacy Association: Newark: DE.

Jung, C. (1971). *Collected works of C.G. Jung, Volume 6: Psychological types.* Princeton: Princeton University Press.

Jung, C. & Campbell, J. *The portable Jung* (1971). NY: Viking/Penguin

Pearson Education Workshop given in St. Louis. (June, 2012). NY, NY: Pearson Publishers.

APPENDIX A
TEACHER INTERVIEWS

CARLA'S CLASSROOM: AN INTERVIEW ABOUT USING TRADE BOOKS IN THE CLASSROOM.

Carla has an exceptional individualized reading program that promotes interest, critical thinking, passion, and life-long reading skills.

One of the best reading programs in an elementary classroom that Dianne saw was in Carla's fourth grade class at a preschool through sixth grade school in a Midwestern city. Dianne was a Reading Specialist at the School. After Dianne got her Ph.D., she decided she needed to go back into a K-12 classroom to make sure that she wasn't an "ivory tower" professor and that she could still relate to what students need for best literacy practice in all subjects. She was fortunate to get a job as a Reading Specialist (now usually called Literacy Coach) in a non-traditional pre-school-Grade 6 setting. The school was a multiple-intelli-

gences school and the director was good friends with Howard Gardner. Although she did not work with pre-school or kindergarten children, she was responsible for 30 students from first through sixth grade. She learned a great deal from each group but had the most success in Carla's fourth-grade classroom. Carla was the only one who believed a reading specialist needed to work with her entire class, not just the students on the specialist's caseload. Although used with fourth grade students, Carla's Reading Program could work well with all subjects in middle school, high school, and beyond.

Carla developed her own program, where students did not use textbooks. Instead, her entire reading program was based on trade books. Carla did still use certain books to teach to the entire class, such as *The Westing Game* and *The Incredible Journey*. But other than that, students were free to choose their own reading material. However, they were challenged to not only select books that were easy for them to read, but to also choose "medium" and "challenging" books each semester in order to meet the requirements (or to meet their goal). Carla worked with small groups while the other students read their books silently or listened to the book on tape, Groups were chosen in a variety of ways:

- according to reading abilities
- according to reading interests,
- according to diverse groups with different reading skills and abilities
- according to social interactions

On the first day that Carla introduced Dianne to the classroom, she told the class that Dianne would be working with all of the students. Dianne actually had three students on her caseload out of Carla's 20 students in the class, but none of the students except the ones who were on her caseload ever knew which ones were under her supervision. Instead, the majority of the class thought she worked with each of them.

One thing happened to Dianne that helped her succeed with this group. It occurred right from the beginning. After Carla introduced Dianne and told the class that she would be working with all students individually while she, Carla, conducted her reading groups, Dianne walked over to one of the students and began talking to her about what she was reading. Unknown to Dianne, this particular student was brilliant and a highly successful reader. When the students all saw that Dianne was working with her, they naturally assumed she would be working with every one of them, which, in fact, she did. However, Dianne also made sure that while she was in the room, she always touched bases with her three caseload students. What was interesting was the way every student in that room wanted to discuss their books with her. Because they had chosen their reading material themselves, they were interested and enthusiastic about what they were reading.

Often, after Carla had worked with a reading group or held a book conference, students would choose to read the book described by someone else in the group. Research indicates that students are more influenced by their peers than they are their teachers, and Dianne's experience in that classroom verified this finding. In addition, one of the students who was on her caseload was friends with another boy who was extremely intelligent and an avid reader. When his friend chose to read Jurassic Park, Dianne's student read it as well. Even though the book was at a difficult level for him, he managed to read each book and understand it. It may have taken him longer, and he sometimes talked with his friend about certain events for clarity, but he was able to read the books.

Studies indicate students will rise to the level of a teacher's expectations, but in this case, Dianne discovered that her student was able to raise his reading level based on his friend's interests, which were similar to his own, even though the material was harder for him. The boy's friend, who read widely and read material far above his grade level, was at a fluent level, whereas Dianne's student was at an instructional level. However, his friend was able to give him more instructions than Dianne could, because he trusted his friend's knowledge and understanding far more than he trusted hers. After all, he had been friends with the other boy for years and Dianne had just come onto the scene. What Dianne did in this case was to converse with both boys about what they were reading. Even though they may have been in different places, by having the avid reader first describe his chapter, my student was given a type of "pre-reading" strategy that would help him to comprehend the chapter when he came upon it later. In addition, Dianne's student demonstrated his comprehension of the chapter he read while summarizing it in his own words.

When Dianne had the opportunity to observe Carla working with her reading groups, she could see that Carla was a wide reader herself. In that class, as in most classes, the reading levels of the students varied widely, from second grade through the tenth grade level, as measured on a standardized test. However, just because students may be able to read at an advanced level, it does not mean they should be reading all books at that level. Many of the advanced level books are intended for older, more mature readers. Dianne learned how important this concept was when she brought in a difficult mystery for one of the students on her caseload to read. He was actually a good reader but had ADHD and needed to stay on task. He showed the book to Carla after Dianne left the room and Carla informed Dianne that the material was much too advanced in content for him to read at his age.

A big part of Carla's success in her reading program was using trade books. Trade books are any nonfiction or fiction books that are not textbooks. In teaching other subjects, Carla did not use textbooks, but relied on a variety of trade books to teach every subject. When students took their national and state tests, they did very well, which indicates that teachers need not be required to use textbooks to "teach to the test." Carla and Dianne did teach the students test-taking skills, which was quite different from the common practice many teachers are forced to do because of the legislation in the United States that demands increased test scores for determining teacher compensation and even hiring. Once Carla's students learned to master test-taking skills, they did not need to face months of boring lectures just to meet national and state testing guidelines.

AN INTERVIEW WITH BRIAN: USING OTHER LITERACIES IN THE CLASSROOM

Brian Teaches Social Studies in a high school where English is not the first language of 40% of his students.

Last summer, Brian took the graduate *Reading in the Content Area* three credit course from Dianne. Based on the various assignments from this class, Brian was able to take what he had learned and apply it to his students.

Brian has been teaching social studies at a public high school in the southern part of a Midwestern city for several years. He teaches social studies and 40 percent of his students are Bosnian, which mean English is their second language. Their understanding of the language ranges from good to poor. The remaining 60 percent of the students are a diverse group, consisting of African-Americans, Asians, Caucasians and Vietnamese.

READABILITY

Brian applied what he had learned from the readability section of his textbook. He strongly suspected that his textbook was far too difficult for his students, and the readability study validated his viewpoint.

Although his American Social Studies textbook was adequate for his junior students, the textbook for the American Government class for sophomores was far too difficult. Therefore, Brian essentially created his own materials. He used internet sources for help, but he wrote his lessons based on reading strategies that work.

PROCESS FOR USING OTHER LITERACIES

One of the strategies we used in our Reading in the Content Course was the Jigsaw method. Brian has used this strategy successfully with his students. His students needed to understand the Preamble to the Constitution. Dianne remembers having to memorize the Preamble in the fourth or fifth grade, which she could easily do, but she did not know what all of the words meant. Instead of a memorization requirement, Brian takes each line and breaks it into parts. He defines and prepares the six essential components of the Preamble and asks the students to tell him what words they find difficult. As many of these students are ELL's, they circle words they do not understand, such as **form, establish, tranquility, promote, welfare, liberty, and posterity.** Students are divided into four or five groups; their assignment is to discuss what they think is meant by the heading they are given. Students are free to use their text (although complicated) in addition to other material Brian has prepared for them, which describes each component in simpler, more effective and understandable explanations. He has the students then find the 6 parts of the constitution that list the goals he has given the students and has them put each definition into their own words. He divides the students into six groups and gives each group about six minutes max to complete their description in their own words. Then he selects a "leader" who goes to each group and teaches them the group's meaning of the major point assigned. Brian uses different methods of selecting the Discussion Leader such as:

Whose birthday is the closest to the current day?

Whose birthday is the furthest from the current day?

Who is wearing the most of the color red (Brian changes the colors)

Brian places a time limit on this activity because the period only lasts 45 minutes and also because he wants his students to stay on task. After the students in each group have discussed the component, they are asked to record it on their chart. By using this random method of selection, none of the students know who will be chosen; therefore, they all need to thoroughly understand the material they have summarized and be able to explain it to the other groups. When Dianne asked him how the Discussion Leader was able to obtain the information, Brian explained that this process is done during the review period. Instead of having each leader stand up and relate the information again, another student is randomly selected according to the various methods described above. While each of the students now chosen explains the main elements of their component, the original Discussion Leader has time to record everyone's summary. Brian reiterates that students do not use the textbook, because it is far too difficult. Instead, they use the information he has created, based on a variety of internet sources.

ADVICE FOR ALL HIGHER EDUCATION INSTRUCTORS

Brian attended a public university and says he got an excellent education. However, he said that the professors never told him that he would need to create his own "textbook" or materials to accommodate the diversity of learners, ranging from ELL's to many other cultural groups. Dianne and Paula realized that they need to be more vigilant about explaining to students how much time, effort, motivation, enthusiasm, and knowledge needs to go into originating the curriculum themselves. Even when Dianne and Paula use good textbooks, they develop major additional material for their courses. They also always use Before, During, and After Reading strategies. If the goal of higher education teachers is to help their students become life-long learners, teaching them how to make information interesting, relevant, applicable, and useful to students is important. This means investing time and energy as Brian does, but the results are invaluable. When students know what they are learning and why they are learning it, they are much more willing to participate. Although some students may be shy and not wish to get up in front of others, Brian says all students need to have this skill, which is why everyone in the class eventually leads others in class discussions.

www.ingramcontent.com/pod-product-compliance
Lightning Source LLC
Chambersburg PA
CBHW060745240426
43665CB00054B/2969